GPH BOOK

For

Bachelor of Computer Applications (BCA)

For

IGNOU, IP University, Delhi University, CCS University, JMI University, B. M. V. Open University (KOTA), M. P. Bhoj Open University(M.P.), Tamilnadu Open University, YCM Open University (Maharashtra), Mahatma Gandhi University (Kottyam), M. D.University, and all other Indian Universities.

WINDOWS PROGRAMMING

CS-65

GULLYBABA PUBLISHING HOUSE (P) Ltd.

AN ISO 9001:2008 CERTIFIED CO.

GullyBaba Publishing House (P) Ltd.
2525 / 193, Ist Floor, Onkar Nagar-A,
Tri Nagar, Delhi-110035
Ph: 9350849407, 9312235086, 011-27387998

E-mail: info@gullybaba.com
info@degreewala.com
WebSite: www.gullybaba.com,
www.doeacconline.com

2010 Edition

Author : Seema Bhatia, Dinesh Verma

Price : 220/-

Preface

This book is mainly targeted for the exam of Windows Programming for all Universities. It has been introduced in market after seeing the huge demand of ready to grasp material for exams with high level of quality, and its un-availability in market. We the GullyBaba Publishing House took a step ahead to publish the quality material focusing on exams at the same time giving you indepth knowledge about the subject.

GPH Book is the pioneer effort that provides a unique methodology so as to perform better in exams. If your goal is to attain higher grade use this powerful study tool independently or along with your text.

*On the Web : **www.gullybaba.com** is the vital resource for your exams acting as catalyst to boost up your preparation. Now you can access us on the net through **www.doeacconline.com**, **www.ignouonline.com**, and **www.astrologyeverywhere.com.***

***Feedback about the book can be sent at* cs65writers@gullybaba.com.**

Constructive criticism is always welcome as it will add to our knowledge. You can email at cs65@gullybaba.com.

New Delhi

INDEX

WINDOWS PROGRAMMING

CS-65

STUDY MATERIAL

QUESTION PAPERS

Feedback is the breakfast of Champions.

Ken Blanchard

You can Help other students.
"Inform any error or mistake in this book."

We and Universe
will reward you for Your Kind act.

Email at : feedback@gullybaba.com
or
WhatsApp on 9350849407

Chapter - 1

Introduction of Visual Basic

Introduction : Visual Basic is high level programming language evolved from the earlier DOS version called BASIC (Beginner's All-purpose symbolic Instruction Code). The natural evolution or Basic was Visual Basic, which was created by Microsoft Corporation in 1991.

Until Visual Basic appeared, developing Microsoft Window-based-application was a difficult and cumbersome process. Visual Basic greatly simplifies Window application development. Since 1991, six versions have been released with the latest-Visual Basic 6-appearing in September 1998.

Visual Basic 6.0 is a member of the Visual Basic 6.0 family of development product, which include :

• Visual Basic 6.0

- Visual C++
- Visual FoxPro
- Visual InterDev
- Visual J++
- Visual SourceSafe
- MSDN Library

Visual Basic 6.0 is available in three editions :

(a) Standard Edition is used to write application for Windows 95 and Windows 98 and Windows NT. It contains standard controls like: List box, Combo box, Check box and so on.

(b) Professional Edition is used by professional programmers, it includes all the features of standard edition plus custom controls, crystal report, online help, Data Access Objects (DAO) and other tools.

(c) Enterprise Edition is used to build client-server application, it include all the features of professional edition plus source code control, Remote Data Access Component Manager and Data Explorer.

Understanding of Visual Basic?

The "Visual" part refers to the method used to create the graphical user interface (GUI). Rather than writing numerous lines or code to describe the appearance and location of interface elements, you simply add pre-built objects into place on screen.

While writing the program you are able to see how your program will look like during run time. This is great advantage over other programming languages. You are able to change experiment with your design until you are satisfied with feature like color, size, images that are included in the program.

Visual Basic is an event driven programming also. It is governed by event processor due to its Window Interface the user may click on a certain object randomly, so each object has to be programmed independently to be able to response to those actions (event). It is a beautiful combination of object oriented and event driven programming, that support visual effects i.e. GUI effects.

Visual Basic Interface : A user interface is a mean by which a user interact with an application. The data entry screen that accepts input for product order is an example. A well designed user interface on effective means of making an application user friendly because it enable the user to tell the computer what comes next.

Types of User Interface : There are two types of User Interface:
(a) CUI, and
(b) GUI

• **Character User Interface (CUI) :** In CUI, we interact with application by relying in commands. Here we need to remember all the commands and the complete syntax. Examples of CUI is OS, MS-DOS, UNIX etc.

• **Graphical User Interface (GUI) :** A GUI, on the other hand provide a graphical way or interacting with a system. GUI are easy to learn and use, as we do not have to remember the commands or syntax. Most of the commands can be executed using the mouse. An example of GUI is MS-Windows.

Features of VB : VB programming environment provides all features that are required to develop a graphical user interface as ready-to-use components. Some of them are listed below :

• It is successor of BASIC language.
• VB supports event driven programming.
• **Common Programming Platform :** VB provides a common programming platform across all MS-Office applications.
• **Quick Development :** VB offers many tools that support and provide easy way to develop applications.
• **Wizards :** VB also provides many wizards (instructions) that can automate task or even automate coding.
• Full set of objects you draw the application.
• Full array of mathematical, string handling and graphics functions.
• Sequential and random access file support.
• Useful debugger and error handling facilities.
• Powerful database access tools.
• Can handle fixed and dynamic variables and control arrays.
• Active X support
• N-tier Architecture.

Note : A n-tier Architecture uses business rules handling objects for data access. It has multiple server handling business services that are used by most of the modern enterprises.

Visual Basic Environment : The working environment in VB integrates many different functions. Such as designing, editing, compiling and debugging with in a common environment.

(a) Start-up Visual Basic :

(1) Click at Start button.

(2) Click at Programs → Microsoft Visual Studio → Microsoft Visual Basic. This will open New Project dialog, which is the startup dialog. From this dialog, you can select the desired project type.

A project in VB is a collection of several different types of files that make up your program. Application is also a related term that is final program used by people.

(b) Concept of VB projects : In Visual Basic, a project is a group of all the files that are included in your program. These might include form, module (block of code not attached to a form), graphics and Active X controls, in which each them save as individual file.

Common file type in VB are:

File Type	Description
FRM	Form
BAS	Module
FRX	Automatically generated file for every graphic
OCX	Active X control
CLS	Class Module
VBP	Visual Basic Project

VB projects : A project is VB is a collection of different types of files. Project file has the extension .VBP.

Various types of projects that you can create are :

• **Standard EXE :** Standard EXE is used for creating a new or typical application/ project. VB show, the working environment referred to as Integrated Development Environment or IDE.

Visual Basic IDE consists of following elements:

(1) Title Bar : It is top most bar displaying the title of the project (Project1- Microsoft Visual Basic [Design]).

(2) Menu Bar and Pull-down Menus : The horizontal menu displayed below the title bar is menu bar and each option on the menu bar has a drop-down list on items known as pull-down menus. (File, Edit, View, Project, Format etc.).

(3) Standard Toolbar : A toolbar is a bar that displays icons for commonly used tasks and quick assess the features.

(4) Form : Forms are the main part of the project are used to display various controls that form the user interface. Forms are used to display things like Labels, Graphics, Controls, etc.

(5) Toolbox : A toolbox is a window that displays a set of tools that may be used to place controls on a form. The buttons on the toolbox depict controls.

(6) Form Designer : Form designer window is the form window in design form. In this designer window you can see grid of dots which disappear at run time. Different toolbox controls are placed on form.

(7) Project Explorer: The project explorer shows the list of forms and modules in a project.

(8) Properties Window: The properties window lists the properties of a selected control or for the form. A property is a characteristic of an object such as its size, its caption or its colour etc.

(9) Form Layout Window: This window show how big a form is in relation to the screen.

(10) Context Menus: These are shortcut menus that contain shortcuts to frequently performed actions. It open after right click on object.

(11) Code Editor Window: The code editor window is where you write VB code for your application. A separate code editor window is created for each form or control that you create in your application.

Various window can be opened through View menu and closed through Close button.

To exit Visual Basic we use follow:

(1) File → Exit

(a) Alt + F4

(b) Alt + Q

(2) Active X Exe: It is a project type for creating application that can either run as stand-alone application or can be executed through automation (locally or remotely) like MS-Word. Unlike Active X DLLs, Active EXEs do not run-in process. It run in its own private address space and contain one class module by default.

(3) Active X DLL: VB allow the programmer to create another type of COM-based object which is not executable by itself but used by another application. This Active X component (unit of executable code) is called Active X dynamic link library (DLL). Active X DLL leaded in process. So, it is called in-process component.

(4) Active X Control: An Active X control is basic element of user interface like Text box, Check box, Command button etc. It is an extension to the Visual Basic Toolbox when you add it becomes part of the development and run-time environment and provide new functionality for your application.

(5) VB Application Wizards: VB application wizard is a new fully functional application from which you build a more complex application. This application wizards used predefined visual interface – Multiple Document Interface (MDI), Single Document Interface (SDI).

(6) VB Wizards Manager: It is used for building your own wizard. A wizard is a sequence of dialog window that collect information from the user. After the user fills all the demanded information, the wizard proceeds to carry out a specific task.

(7) Active X Document DLL: It is used for creating your own Active X document in DLL (Dynamic Link Library) form. Its programs are modified for working with web browser.

(8) Active X Document EXE: It is used for creating Active X document is EXE (Executable) form. These are the programs that also have been modifies to work within web browser such as Internet Explorer.

(9) Add-in: Visual Basic allow you to select and manage add-ins which are extensions to Visual Basic. These extensions add special source code and control capabilities.

(10) Data Project: A data project is a collection of one or more data connections that enable you to access your server database when you create database through ODBC or OLEDB.

(11) DHTML Application: A DHTML application is a program that you design within the DHTML page. Designer in Visual Basic IDE and program in Visual Basic, but it runs as HTML in Internet Explorer.

(12) IIS Application: The software used on physical computer to make it a server that can speak the protocol (set of rules) of the Internet and respond accordingly is called Internet Server Software that is manufactured by Microsoft Internet Information Server (IIS).

(13) VB Pro/Enterprise Edition Controls: It simply creates a new standard EXE project and loads all the tools of the Professional/Enterprise Edition of VB.

Visual Basic Application Modes: A Visual Basic application works in three modes:

(1) Design mode

(2) Run mode

(3) Break mode

Visual Basic Data Types: Data types are means to identify the type of data and associated operation with it.

Data type	Storage size	Range
Byte	1 byte	0 to 255
Boolean	2 bytes	True or False
Integer	2 bytes	-32.768 to 32.767
Long (Integer)	4 bytes	-2,147,483,648 to 2,147,483,647
Single (Single-precision floating –point)	4 bytes	-3.402823E38 to –1.401298E-45 for negative value 1.401298E-45 to 3.402823E38 for positive value
Double (double-precision floating -point) currency	8 bytes	-1.79769131486231E308 to –4.94065645841247E-324 for negative; 4.94065645841247E-324 to 1.7969313486232E308 for positive values.
Currency	8 bytes	-922,337,203,685,477.5815 to 922,337,203,685,477.5807
Decimal	14 bytes	—
Date	8 bytes	Jan 1, 100 to Dec 31, 9999
Object	4 bytes	Any object reference
String (var-length)	10 bytes	+ String length 0 to approx. 2 billion.
String (Fixed-length)	Length of string	1 to approximately 65,400
Variant (with number)	16 bytes	Any numeric value up to range of a Double.
Variant (with characters)	22 bytes + String length	The range of each element is the same as the range of its data type.
User defined (Using type)	Number required by elements	

Chapter - 2

Programming in Visual Basic

Variables: VB allows us to use variables for temporarily storing data at run time. A variable has a name and datatype. The variable is used to access and manipulate the value of the variables. The datatype of a variable determines the type of data that the variable can store.

Declaring Variables: Declaring variable means telling the program about it (variable) in advance.
SYNTAX
Dim <varname> [As < Datatype>][<varnam>][As <Datatype>]
Here, Dim and As is the keywords (Predefined words), and <varname> is the variable name.
For example:
Dim Salary as integer

Dim name as string
Dim amt as currency

Defining Named Constants: We can also define own named constants for use in VB. The format for defining is:
SYNTAX
Const <constant name> = <value>
For example:
Const PT = 3.14159

Variable Scope: Parts of program is which a variable is accessible, is known as its scope.
There can be three different types of scope in VB.
· Private (or local) scope
· Module scope
· Public scope

(1) Private or Local Scope: A variable that can be used only in one procedure in which is declared is said to have private scope like an example:

```
Private Sub From_Load(1)
Dim Value1 as currency
Value1 = 8912.5
Form1.caption = "variable scope"
End Sub
```

Here, variable value1 is declared inside Form_Load(1) procedure using Dim statement. This variable can be used only inside Forn_Load(1) procedure. Therefore value1 has private or Local scope within procedure Form_Load( ).

(2) Module Scope: A module is a place to store commonly used things. In VB these are three kinds of modules: form module where event procedures for all control placed in it. A standard module stores the commonly used variables, constant and procedure etc. And a class module store code to create new objects of OOPS.
A variable that is available inside a module is said to have module scope.

(3) Public Scope: The variable available to all modules and procedures in an application are said to have Public Scope. It is also called global variable of global scope.

Operators in Visual Basic: Operators are the symbols or words that trigger on action on some data.
The data on which operators operate are called operands.
Operators in VB can be divided into following categories:

(1) Arithmetic Operator: These are symbols that are used to perform arithmetic operation variables.

Operators	Uses	Description
+	Used to add two numbers	x + y y = A + B etc.
-	Used to subtract two numbers	x = y – z A = z – x etc
*	Used to multiply two numbers	Z = x * y
^	Used to raise the number to the power of another number called exponent	X = y ^ z
/	Used to divide two numbers and return floating point	Z = x / y
\	Used to divide two numbers and returns an integer result	Z = x \ y
Mod	Used to divide two numbers for remainder	Z = x Mod y

(2) Comparison Operator: These operators are used to compare two value and perform an action based on the result of the comparison.

Operators	Uses	Description
<	Used to check whether val1 is less than val2 (val1 < val2)	Dim result as Boolean x = 20, y = 25 Result = x < y is true
>	Used to check whether val1 is greater than val2 (val1 > val2)	Dim result as Boolean x = 20, y = 25 Result = x > y is false
<=	Used to check whether val1 is less than or equal to val2 (val1 <= val2)	Dim result as Boolean x = 20, y = 25 Result = x <= y is true
>=	Used to check whether val1 is greater than or equal to val2 (val1 >= val2)	Dim result as Boolean x = 20, y = 25 Result = x >= y is false
=	Used to check whether val1 is equal to val2 (val1 = val2)	Dim result as Boolean x = 20, y = 25 Result = x = y is false
<>	Used to check whether val1 is not equal to val2 (val1 <> val2)	Dim result as Boolean x = 20, y = 25 Result = x <> y is true

(3) Logical Operator: The logical operator are used to generally combine two or more checking condition and return a Boolean value.

Operators	Uses	Description
AND	If both the operand condition are true, it returns true otherwise false	Dim res as Boolean x = 30, y = 50 1) Res = x >= 30 AND x < y return true 2) Res = x < 30 AND y = 50 is false
OR	Returns true if at least one of the operand condition is true otherwise false	Dim res as Boolean x = 30, y = 50 1) Res = x = 30 OR x < y is true 2) Res = x = 50 OR y > x is true 3) Res = x = 30 OR y = 50 is true both are true
NOT	It returns true if the expression is false	Dim res as Boolean x = 30, y = 50 1) Res = NOT(x = 30) return false 2) Res = NOT(x = 50) return true
XOR	Returns true if one operand condition is true and other is false and same as false condition	Dim res as Boolean x = 30, y = 50 1) Res = (x = 30) XOR y = 60 return true 2) Res = x = 30 XOR y = 50 is false

(4) Concatenation Operators (&): It is used to concatenate two or more strings. For example: “a” & “b” will return “ab”.

```
Dim str1 as string
Dim str2 as string
Dim str3 as string
Dim name as string
str1 = “Mrs.”
str2 = “ANITA”
str3 = “VERMA”
Name = “str1 &” “str2 &” “str3”
Msgbox(Name)
```

Visual Basic Control Structure: Usually, the statement in a program are executed one after another. However, we can control the sequence of execution of statement by using various control statement and Loops.

(1) Decision Structures: The decision structures choose the set-of-instructions for executing depending upon the test condition or Boolean expression truth value, whether the result of test condition is true or false.

The IF Statement: The IF statement of VB comes in various forms.

- **The IF...Then Statement:** This statement test a particular condition that is true or false.

SYNTAX

```
If(Boolean expression) Then
Statement
End If
```

- **The IF...Then...Else Statement:** This is another form of IF that allow for this kind of either or condition by providing an else clause.

SYNTAX

```
If(Boolean expression) Then
line of code execute when true
Else
line of code execute when false
End If
```

- **The IF...Then...ElseIF statement:** This statement is last in the If family of statements. It allows you to test a number of mutually extensive cases and only executes one set of lines of code for the case that is true first.

SYNTAX

```
If(Boolean expression) Then
line of code to execute when true
ElseIf(Boolean expression) Then
.
.
.
Else line of code to execute when all expression are false
EndIf
```

The Select Case: This statement can be used when multiple. If statement become messy and difficult to read and when multiple paths are associated with single condition.

SYNTAX

Select case Expression

Cash value

One ore more VB statement

Cash value

One or more VB statement

Cash value

One or more VB statement

End Select

(2) Looping Structure: Looping structure are used to execute one or more lines of code repeatedly looping is also known as repetition or iteration.

VB offers broadly following three types of looping structure:

1) For…Next

2) Do Loop

a) Do while…Loop

b) Do…Loop while

c) Do Until…Loop

d) Do…Loop Until

3) While…Wend

1) For…Next: You should use this type of loop when you know exactly how many times the code must be repeated.

SYNTAX

For <counter_var> = <start_val> To <end_val> Step <increment_val>

One or more VB statement

Next <counter_var>

2) Do Loop: A Do Loop repeats statements in its body depending upon the given condition result.

a) Do While…Loop: You should use Do While loop when you want to test a condition first and if the condition evaluates to true then only you want to repeat the statement.

SYNTAX

Do While (<comparison_test>)

One or more VB statement

Loop

b) Do…Loop While: This structure works little differently unlike the first Do loop, the loop body in this loop is executed first before <comparison_test>. If the test is true, VB repeats the loop body otherwise exists the loop. Do_Loop_While execute the loop body at least once.

SYNTAX
Do
One or more VB statement
LoopWhile (<comparison_test>)

c) Do Until...Loop: This loop is similar to Do While Loop but with a little difference. The keyword until means that as long as the comparison test is Not True, the loop repeats.

SYNTAX
Do Until (<comparison_test>)
One or more VB statement
Loop

d) Do...Loop Until: This statement the <comparison_test> is evaluated at the end of the iteration.

SYNTAX
Do
One or more VB statement
Loop Until (<comparison_test>)

3) While...Wend: This is same as Do While...Loop, the While execute at least once.

SYNTAX
While (<comparison_test>)
VB statement
Wend

(3) The Exiting from Loop: Sometime, you may need to exit from a loop even though, its terminating condition has not reached. In such a case, you can use Exit statement.

SYNTAX
Exit For 'For exiting from a For Loop
Exit Do 'For exiting from a Do Loop

(4) Arrays: An Array is a collection of variable of the same type that are referenced by a common name.

Array allow us to refer to a series of variable by the same name and to use a number (an index) to tell them apart. This help us to create smaller and simpler code in many situation because we can set up loops that deal efficiently with any number of cases by using the index number.

In Visual Basic, there are two types of arrays: a fixed d-size array or static array that always remains the same size, and a dynamic array whose size change at run time.

Static Array:

SYNTAX

Dim arrayName(Max Index In Array) As Data Type

Dynamic Array: A dynamic array can be resized at any time, they help you to manage memory efficiently.

There are two processes:

1) First, declare the array must be in same way but without a number of elements specified.

Dim books( ) As String

2) Allocate the actual number of elements with a ReDim statement.

ReDim preserve books(99)

The ReDim statement can appear only in a procedure. Unlike the Dim and static statement, ReDim is an executable statement.

For Each…Next Loop: This similar to a For…Next loop, but it repeats a group of statement for each elements in a collection of object. This is helpful if we don't know the element in dynamic array.

SYNTAX

For Each element In group

Statement

Next element

Chapter - 3

VB Modules

Q1. What is form module?

Ans. A project is made up of modules, such as form *modules*. Form modules consist of small pieces called *procedures*. Form modules (.frm file name extension) can contain textual descriptions of the form and its controls, including their property setting.

Q2. What is standard module?

Ans. Standard modules (.bas file name extension) are containers for procedures and declarations commonly accessed by other modules within the application. They can contain global available to the whole application or module-level declarations of variables, constants, types, external procedures and global procedures.

Q3. What is class module?

Ans. Class modules (.cls file name extension) are the foundation of object-oriented programming in Visual Basic. You can write code in class modules to create new objects. These new object can include your own customized properties and methods. Actually, forms are just class modules that can have controls placed on them and can display form windows.

Q4. What are the major benefits for using procedures in VB?

Ans. The major benefits are:

• Procedures allow you to break your programs into discrete logical units, each of which you can debug more easily than an entire program without procedures.

• Procedures used in one program can act as building blocks for other programs, usually with little or no modification.

Q5. What are the procedure types in Visual Basic?

Ans. There are the following procedure types in Visual Basic:

• General procedure which tells the application how to perform a specific task.

• *Event procedures* which respond the events (i.e., pressing a button, etc.)

• *Visual Basic procedures* which are provided by Microsoft to perform common tasks (i.e., Format$, IIF, LoadPicture etc.)

• Sub procedures which allows programmers to create their own procedures (called **Sub** procedures and **Function** procedures) to meet the unique requirements of the problems they solve. The sub procedure do not return a value.

• Function procedures, is just like the sub procedure but function procedure return a value.

• Property procedures can return and assign values and set references to objects.

Q6. What is a Sub procedure? Write its syntax.

Ans. A Sub procedure is a block of code that is executed in response to an event. By breaking the code in a module into Sub procedures, it becomes much easier to find or modify the code in your application. The syntax for a Sub procedure is:

[Private|Public] [Static] Sub *procedurename* (*arglist*)
[*statements*]

[Exit Sub]
[*statements*]
End Sub

Q7. What is the use of Call statement?

Ans. The Call statement transfers control to a **Sub** procedure or **Function** procedure. You are not required to use the **Call** keyword when calling a procedure. However, if you use the **Call** keyword to call a procedure that requires arguments, *argmentlist* must be enclosed in parentheses.

Q8. What is an event procedure? Explain with example.

Ans. When an object in Visual Basic recognizes that an event has occurred, it automatically invokes the event procedure the object and the code, event procedures are said to be attached to forms and controls.

An event procedure for a control combines the control's actual name (specified in the Name property), and underscore (_), and the event name. For instance, if you want a command button named cmdPlay to invoke an event procedure when it is clicked, use the procedure cmdPlay_Click.

Q9. Write one important difference between function procedure and sub procedure.

Ans. Function procedures and **Sub** procedures share the characteristics, with one important difference:

Function procedures *return* a value (i.e., give a value back) to the caller, whereas **Sub** procedures do not.

Q10. How can you to terminate a sub procedure and a function procedure?

Ans. Exit Sub can appear as many times as needed, anywhere within the body of a Sub procedure. Exit Function can appear as many times as needed, anywhere within the body of a Function procedure.

Exit Sub and Exit Function are useful when the procedure has done everything it needs to do and can return immediately. Statements **Exit Sub** and **Exit Function** alter the flow of control.

Executing **Exit Sub** in a **Sub** procedure causes an immediate exit from that procedure. Control is returned to the caller and the next statement in sequence after the call is executed.

Statement **Exit Function** cause immediate exit from a **Function** procedure. Control is returned to the caller and the next statement an sequence after the call is executed.

Q11. State the difference between Function vs. Procedure.

Ans. A *Function* is a set of statements that performs a specific task within a program and return either a number or a string value. Visual Basic has a number of functions. A function begins with Function statement and ends with an *End Function* statement. A function may also accept arguments. These arguments are enclosed in parenthesis ( ) following the function name.

A *Procedure* is a sequence of code statements that performs a specific task within a program but return no explicit value. These statements are executed as a unit. A *Sub* Procedure begins with a *Sub* statement and ends with a *End Sub* statement. Sub procedure performs actions but do not return any values whereas function procedures perform action and return values.

A *Function* or *Procedure* tells an application what and how to perform a specific task when an event is generated. Once the function or procedure is define it must be explicitly involved by the applicator. An event procedure remains idle until called upon to respond to events caused by the user. You can place a function or procedure in a form module, standard module or class module.

Q12. Write the scope rule to use a variable in modules.

Ans. To make a module level variable available to other modules, use the Public keyword to declare the variable. The values in public variables are available to all procedures in your application. Like all module level variables, public variables are declared in the Declarations section at the top of the module. For example,

Public intTemp As Integer

Chapter - 4

Standard Library Functions

Types of Functions :

(1) String Functions

(2) Arithmetic Functions and

(3) Calendar Functions

Concepts of Characters and Strings: Characters are the fundamental building blocks of Visual Basic source programs. Every program is composed of a sequence of characters that – when grouped together meaningfully – is interpreted by the computer as a series of instructions used to accomplish a task. Each character is represented internally as a small integer in the range 0 to 255 (e.g., 65 represents the uppercase letter **A**, 66 represents the uppercase letter **B**, 97 represents the lowercase letter **a**, 98 represents the lowercase letter **b** etc.).

A string is a series of characters treated as a single unit. A string may include letters, digits and various special characters such as '+', '-', '*', '/', '$' and others. A string in Visual Basic is of data type **String**. *String literals* or *string constants* in Visual Basic are written as a sequence of characters in double quotation marks as follows:

"Dinesh Verma" (a name)
"12345, Pkt-10, S.Ext" (a street address)
"South Ext. New Delhi" (a city and state)
"(011) 22233 – 333" (a telephone number)

String manipulations inside the computer actually involve the manipulation of the appropriate numeric codes (i.e., the small integers we have been discussing) and not the characters themselves. When a computer compares two strings, it actually compares the underlying numeric codes that make up the characters in the strings.

From this point forward, we shall refer to string values (or string constants) simply a strings. Visual Basic also provides for *string variables* that may contain different strings at different times during a particular execution of a program. The dollar sign **$**, is the type declaration character for a **String**.

Data type String: There are two kinds of strings:
(a) variable length
(b) fixed length strings

• A variable length string can contain up to approximately 2 billion (2^31) characters.

• A fixed length string can contain 1 to approximately 6.

By default, **String** variables represent variable length strings that grow and shrink dynamically based on the strings that are assigned to them, as in the lines

Dim anyStr as String
anyStr = "New Delhi"

that declares **anyStr** as a **String** and assign **anyStr** the string **"New Delhi"**.
Fixed length strings are declared as follows:

Dim *variableName* **As String** * size

Concatenation of String with & and +: A string can be made by concatenating more than one string into one string. This process, called *string concatenation*, and can be made by using a *plus sign (+)* or an *ampersand (&)*.

The **&** operator is used to force string concatenation of two expressions. The syntax as:

result = expression1 **&** *expression2*

The **&** operator syntax has these parts listed in Listing.

The & operators part description.

Part	Description
result	Required; any String or Variant variable.
expression1	Required; any expression.
expression2	Required; any expression.

Category 1:

String Functions: String manipulation features of the Visual Basic language permit the programmer to write program the process letters, words, sentences, names, addresses, descriptive data and special symbols (such as '+', '-', '*', '/' '$' etc.). The following are the some of string function as discussed.

(1) Space( ) and Strings Function: The functions **String $** and **Space $** create strings of a specified number of characters. The Space( ) function returns a **Variant (String)** consisting of the specified number of spaces. The syntax is as:

Space(*number*)

The required *number* argument is the number of spaces you want in the string. The **Space** function is useful for formatting output and clearing data in fixed length strings.

For example,

String$(*number, character*)

The **String$** function syntax has these arguments is listed in Listing.

The part description of String$ function

Part	Description
number	Length of the returned string. If *number* contains **Null, Null** is returned.
character	Character code specifying the character or string expression whose first character is used to build the return string. If *character* contains **Null, Null** is returned.

The following example uses the **String$** function to return repeating character strings of the length specified:

Dim anyString
anyString = String$(5, "*") 'Returns "*****"
anyString = String$(5, 42) 'Returns "*****"
anyString = String$(10, "ABC") 'Returns "AAAAAAAAAA"

(2) Str$( ) Function: The Str$ function is used to convert a numeric value into character or string. Function Str$ is the complement of Val – it converts numbers to strings. The syntax is as:

Str$(*number*)

The required *number* argument is a Long containing any valid numeric expression.

(3) Right$ Function: The **Right$** selects the originated portion of a string. It returns a **Variant (String)** containing a specified number of characters from the right side of a string. The syntax is as:

Right(*string, length*)

The **Right** function syntax has these named arguments listed in Listing.

The part description of Right$ function

Part	Description
string	Required; String expression from which the rightmost characters are returned. If ***string*** contains Null, **Null** is returned.
length	Required; **Variant (Long)**. Numeric expression indicating how many characters to return. If 0, a zero -length string ("") is returned. If greater than or equal to the number of characters in ***string***, the entire string is returned.

(4) Left Function: The **Left$** selects the leftmost portion of a string. It returns a **Variant (String)** containing a specified number of characters from the left side of a string. The syntax as:

Left$*(string, length)*

The **Left$** function syntax has the following named arguments listed in Listing.

The part description of Left$ function

Part	Description
string	Required; String expression from which the rightmost characters are returned. If ***string*** contains Null, Null is returned.
length	Required; **Variant (Long)** . Numeric expression indicating how many characters to return. If 0, a zero -length string ("") is returned. If greater than or equal to the number of characters in ***string***, the entire string is returned.

(5) InStr Function: The **InStr** function is useful for searching through one string, called the *base string*, to determine if it contains another string, called the *search string*. If the second string is found, the starting character location of that string is returned. If the second string is zero length (i.e., it contains no character) the starting position is returned. The syntax is as:

InStr([*start*,]*string1, string2*[, *compare*])

The Listing shows the **InStr** functions arguments description.

The part description of InStr function

Part	Description
start	Optional. Numeric expression that sets the starting position for each search. If omitted, search begins at the first character position. If *start* contains **Null**, an error occurs. The *start* argument is required if *compare* is specified.
string1	Required. String expression being searched.
string2	Required. String expression searched for.
compare	Optional. Numeric value indicating the kind of comparison to use when evaluating substrings. See Settings section for values. If omitted, a binary co mparison is performed.

(6) Mid$ Function : The Mid$ function returns a **Variant (String)** containing a specified number of characters from a string. The syntax is as:

Mid(*string, start*[, *length*])

The **Mid** function syntax has three named arguments listed in Listing.

The part description Mid$ function

Part	Description
string	Required; String expression from which characters are returned. If ***string*** contains Null, **Null** is returned.
start	Required; Long. Character position in ***string*** at which the part to be taken begins. If ***start*** is greater than the number of characters in ***string,*** **Mid** returns a zero -length string ("").
length	Optional; **Variant (Long)** . Number of characters to return. If omitted or if there are fewer than ***length*** characters in the text (including the character at ***start***), all characters from the ***start*** position to the end of the string are returned.

(7) Len Function: The ***Len*** (for "length") function is used to determine the length of a string. It returns a 4 bytes integer containing the number of characters in a string or the number of bytes required to store a variable. The syntax is as:

Len*(string | varname)*

Here, the **Len** function contains the following arguments which is listed in Listing.

Parts of Len function

Part	Description
string	Any valid string expression. If *string* contains Null, Null is returned.
Varname	Any valid variable name. If*varname* contains **Null, Null** is returned. If *varname* is a Variant, **Len** treats if the same as a **String** and always returns the number of characters it contains.

(8) Ltrim$, Rtrim$ and Trim$ Function: Functions ***Ltrim$, Rtrim$*** and ***Trim$*** remove leading spaces at the left side of a string, trailing spaces at the right side of a string, and spaces on both the left and the right side of a string, respectively. These functions are particularly useful for removing extra space characters used to pad a fixed-length string so that the string occupies the total space allocated for it. The syntax for the functions ***Ltrim$, Rtrim$*** and ***Trim$*** are:

Ltrim$*(string)*

Rtrim$*(string)*

Trim$*(string)*

The required *string* argument is any valid string expression. If *string* contains

Null, **Null** is returned.

(9) UCase$ and LCase$ Functions: Functions ***UCase$*** and ***LCase$*** convert strings to all uppercase letters and all lowercase letters, respectively. The ***UCase$*** function returns a **Variant (String)** containing the specified string, converted to uppercase. The syntax for ***UCase$*** function is as:

UCase$(*string*)

Here, the required *string* argument is any valid string expression. If *string* contains Null, **Null** is returned. Only lowercase letters are converted to uppercase; all uppercase letters and non-letter characters remain unchanged. The ***LCase$*** function returns a String that has been converted to lowercase. The syntax for ***ULCase$*** function is as:

LCase$(*string*)

Here, the required *string* argument is any valid string expression. If *string* contains Null, Null is returned. Only uppercase letters are converted to lowercase; all lowercase letters and non-letter characters remain unchanged.

Category 2:

Numeric Functions: Visual Basic supports number of numeric functions which allow the programmer to perform certain common mathematical calculations. These functions are also called mathematical functions.

(1) Sgn( ) Function: This function returns the sign of an integer or number. The syntax is as:

Sgn(*number*)

Here, the required *number* argument can be any valid numeric expression. The listing shows the return values of a Sgn function.

Return values of Sgn function

If *number* is	**Sgn returns**
Greater than zero	1
Equal to zero	0
Less than zero	-1

(2) Val( ) Function : The **Val** function returns the numbers contained in a string as a numeric value of appropriate type. The syntax is as:

Val(*string*)

The required *string* argument is any valid string expression. The **Val** function stops reading the string at the first character it can't recognize as part of a number.

(3) Rnd( ) function: This function returns a Single random number that is always in the range

0 <= Rnd < 1

If Rnd truly produces random numbers, every number between 0 and 1 (but not including 1) has an equal change (or probability) of being chosen each time RND is called. Multiple called to Rnd should not generate any predictable pattern of number. The range of values produced by Rnd is often different from that needed in a specific application. The syntax is as:

Rnd([*number*)]

(4) Int( ) Function: This function returns the integer portion of a number. In the case of a negative number argument, the **Int** function returns the first negative integer less than or equal to the number. The syntax is as:

Int(*number*)

Category 3:

Using the Date, Time and Now Function: As we have discussed the Date and Time function numbers of times in the previous sections, here these two functions are used for managing the time in a much more sophisticated task than most programmer realize. Visual Basic provides many date function and time related function and the **Date** data type to help programmers standardize and ensure the completeness of their dates and times.

(1) Date Function: The **Date** function returns a **Variant (Date)** containing the current system date. The syntax is as:

Date

To set the system date, use the **Date** statement. **Date,** and if the calendar is Gregorian, **Date$** behavior is unchanged by the **Calendar** properly setting.

(2) Day Function: The **Day** function returns a **Variant (Integer)** specifying a whole number 1 and 31, inclusive representing the day of the month. The syntax is as:

Day(date)

The required *date* argument is any Variant, numeric expression, string expression, or any combination, that can represent a date. If *date* contains Null, **Null** is returned.

(3) Month Function: The **Month** function returns a **Variant (Integer)** specifying a whole number between 1 and 12, inclusive, representing the month of the year. The syntax is as:

Month(*date*)

The required *date* argument is any Variant, numeric expression, string expression, or any combination, that can represent a date. If *date* contains Null, **Null** is returned.

(4) Year Function: The **Year** function returns a **Variant (Integer)** containing a whole number representing the year. The syntax is as:

Year(*date*)

The required date argument is any Variant, numeric expression, string expression, or any combination, that can represent a date. If *date* contains Null, **Null** is returned.

(5) Weekday Function: The **Weekday** function returns a **Variant (Integer)** containing a whole number representing the day of the week. The syntax is as:

Weekday(*date*, [***firstdayofweek***])

The **Weekday** function syntax has these named arguments listed in Listing.

The *part description* Weekday function

Part	Description
date	Required. Variant, numeric expression, string expression, or any combination, that can represent a date. If *date* contains Null, **Null** is returned.
firstdayofweek	Optional. A constant that specifies the first day of the week. If not specified, **vbSunday** is assumed.

The ***firstdayofweek*** argument was listed in Listing.

The *firstdayofweek* constants

Constant	Value	Description
vbUseSystem	0	Use NLS API setting.
VbSunday	1	Sunday (default)
vbMonday	2	Monday
vbTuesday	3	Tuesday
vbWednesday	4	Wednesday
vbThursday	5	Thursday
vbFriday	6	Friday
vbSaturday	7	Saturday

(6) Now Function : The **Now** function returns a **Variant (Date)** specifying the current date and time according your computer's system date and time. This syntax is as:

Now

This example uses the **Now** function to return the current system date and time.

Dim Today

Today = **Now** 'Assign current system date and time.'

(7) Time Function: The **Time** function returns a **Variant (Date)** indicating the current system time. The syntax is as:

Time

To set the system time, use the **Time** statement. This example uses the **Time** function to return the current system time.

(8) Hour Function: The **Hour** function returns a **Variant (Integer)** specifying a whole number between 0 to 23, inclusive, representing the hour of the day. The syntax is as:

Hour(*time*)

The required *time* argument is any Variant, numeric expression, string expression, or any combination, that can represent a time. If *time* contains Null, **Null** is returned.

(9) Minute Function: The **Minute** function returns a **Variant (Integer)** specifying a whole number between 0 and 59, inclusive, representing the minute of the hour. The syntax is as:

Minute(*time*)

The required *time* argument is any Variant, numeric expression, string expression, or any combination, that can represent a time. If *time* contains Null, **Null** is returned.

(10) Second Function: The **Second** function returns a **Variant (Integer)** specifying a whole number between 0 and 59, inclusive, representing the second of the minute. The syntax is as:

Second(*time*)

The required *time* argument is any Variant, numeric expression, string expression, or any combination, that can represent a time. If *time* contains Null, **Null** is returned.

MsgBox( ) Function: The **MsgBox** displays a message in a dialog box, waits for the user to click a button, and returns a value indicating which button the user clicked. The general syntax is as:

MsgBox(*prompt*[, *buttons*]], *title*][, *helpfile, context*])

The **MsgBox** function syntax has these arguments listed in Listing.

Part descriptions of MsgBox function

Part	Description
prompt	String expression displayed as the message in the dialog box. The maximum length of *prompt* is approximately 1024 characters, depending on the width of the characters used. If *prompt* consists of more than one line, you c an separate the lines using a carriage return character (**Chr**(13)), a linefeed character (**Chr**(10)), or carriage return-linefeed character combination (**Chr**(13) **&** **Chr**(10)) between each line.
buttons	Numeric expression that is the sum of values specifying the number and type of buttons to display, the icon style to use, the identity of the default button and the modality of the message box. If omitted, the default value for *buttons* is 0.
title	String expression displayed in the title bar of the dialog box. If you omit *title*, the application name is placed in the title bar.
helpfile	String expression that identifies the Help file to use to provide context-sensitive Help for the dialog box. If *helpfile* is provided, *context* must also be provided. Not available on 16-bit platforms.
context	Numeric expression that identifies the Help context number assigned by the Help author to the appropriate Help topic. If *context* is provided, *helpfile* must also be provided. Not available on 16-bit platforms.

Chapter - 5

Menu and MDI Forms in VB

Introduction

Q1. Define the term Development Environment in context of Visual Basic ?

Ans. Learning the ins and outs of the Development Environment before you learn visual basic is somewhat like learning for a test you must know where all the functions belong and what their purpose is.

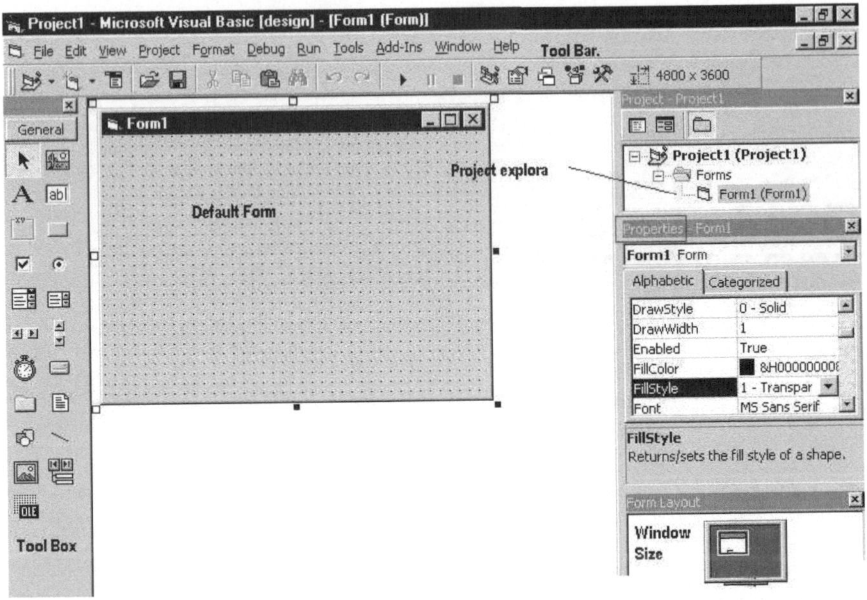

The above diagram shows the development environment with all the important points labelled. Many of Visual basic functions work similar to Microsoft word e.g. the **Tool Bar** and the tool box is similar to other products on the market which work off a single click then drag the width of the object required. The **Tool Box** contains the control you placed on the form window. All of the controls that appear on the **Tool Box** controls on the above picture never runs out of controls as soon as you place one on the form another awaits you on the **Tool Box** ready to be placed as needed.

The project explorer window

The Project explorer window gives you a tree-structured view of all the files inserted into the application. You can expand these and collapse branches of the views to get more or less detail (**Project explorer**). The project explorer window displays forms, modules or other separators which are supported by the visual basic like class'es and Advanced Modules. If you want to select a form on its own simply double click on the project explorer window for a more detailed look. And it will display it where the **Default form** is located.

Properties Window

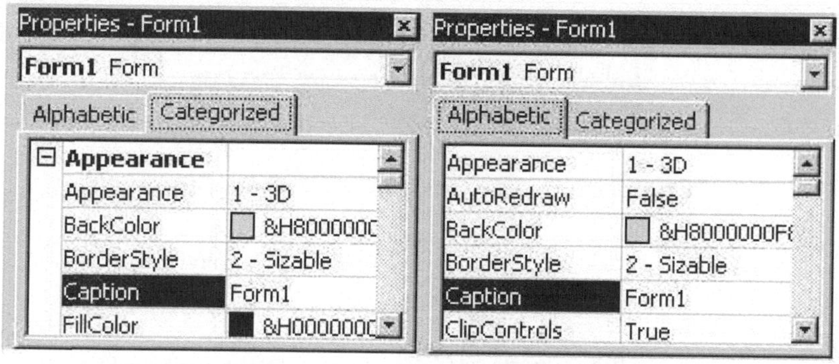

Some programmers prefer the Categorisized view of the properties window. By defaulting, the properties window displays its properties alphabetically (with the exception of the name value) when you click on the categorized button the window changes to left picture.

The Default Layout

A VB project is a collection of the following modules and files. When we start Visual Basic, we are provided with a VB project.

• The **global module(** *that contains declaration and procedures***)**

• The **form module(***that contains the graphic elements of the VB application along with the instruction)*

• The **general module (***that generally contains general-purpose instructions not pertaining to anything graphic on-screen)*

• The **class module***(that contains the defining characteristics of a class, including its properties and methods)*

• The **resource files(***that allows you to collect all of the texts and bitmaps for an application in one place)*

On start up, Visual Basic will displays the following windows :

• The **Blank Form** window

• The **Project** window

• The **Properties** window

It also includes a **Toolbox** that consists of all the controls essential for developing a VB Application. Controls are tools such as boxes, buttons, labels and other objects draw on a form to get **input** or **display output**. They also add visual appeal.

Understanding the tool box.

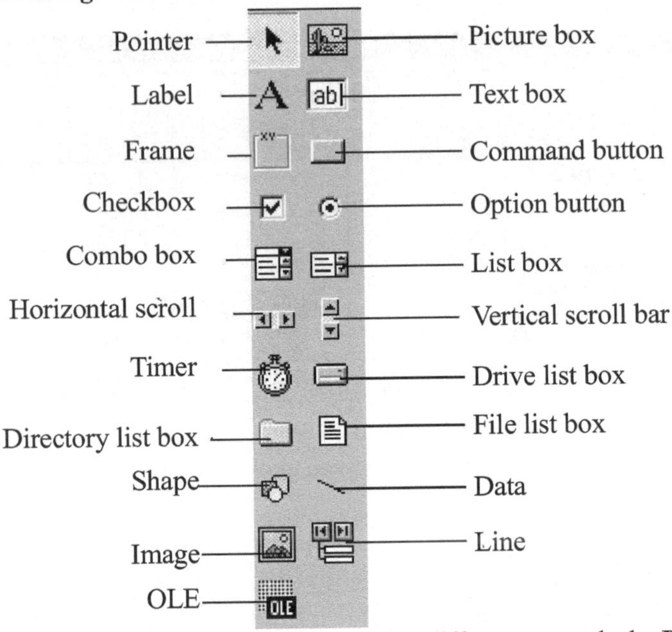

You may have noticed that when you click on different controls the **Properties Window** changes slightly this is due to different controls having different functions. Therefore more options are needed for example if you had a picture then you want to show an image. But if you wanted to open a internet connection you would have to fill in the remote host and other such settings. When you use the command ( ) you will find that a new set of properties come up the following will provide a description and a property.

Q2. How to opening an existing Visual Basic project ?

Ans. Microsoft have included some freebies with visual basic to show its capabilities and functions. Dismantling or modifying these sample projects is a good way to understand what is happening at runtime. These files can be located at your default directory **/SAMPLES/**

To Open these projects choose 'Open Project' from the 'File' menu. Then Double click on the samples folder to open the directory then Double click on any project to load it.

Opening a new visual basic file & Inserting Source code.

From looking at the examples it time to make your own application. Choose

'New Project' from the 'File' menu. Use the blank form1 to design a simple interface for an estate agents database, have some textboxes for names and other details. Insert some controls and make it look professional. Textboxes can be used to store there name and other details, make sure you put a picture box in for a picture of the house.

Now insert the following source code for your application.

```
Private Sub Form_Load()
Picture1.Picture = LoadPicture("C:\Program Files\VB\Graphics\Icons\Misc\MISC42.ICO")
End Sub
```

Q3. Discuss in detail how to Run and view the project in Visual Basic ?

Ans. Once an application is loaded it can be run by click on the icon from the toolbar, to pause press and to terminate use .

Once a project is loaded, the name of the form(s) that it contains is displayed in the project window. To view a form in design mode, select the form required by clicking with the mouse to highlight its name, then clicking on the view form button.

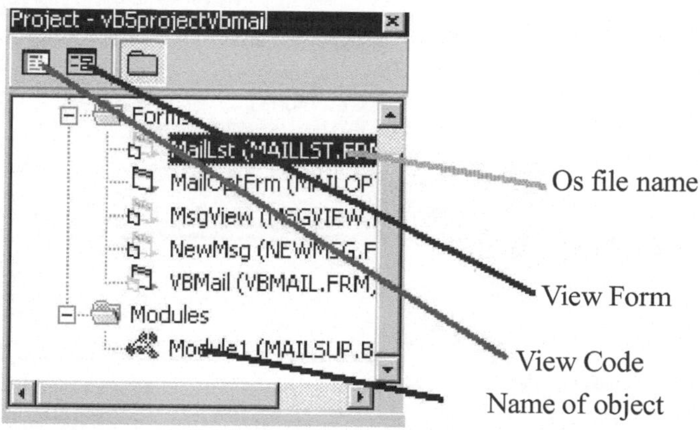

In this example the project has been loaded and the maillist.frm has been selected for viewing. This Ms Mail example project uses 6 forms and 1 modules. In Design mode, when the form is viewed, the code attached to any screen object may be inspected by double clicking on that object. The screen shots below show the interface of the Ms Mail example (.../samples/Comtool/VBMail/MaiLLST.FRM) to view the code for this form select from the project window item.

```
Private Sub SetupOptionForm(BasePic As Control)
BasePic.Top = 0
BasePic.Left = 0
BasePic.Visible = True
BasePic.enabled = True
OKBt.Top = BasePic.Height + 120
Me.width = BasePic.Width + 120
Me.Heigh = OkBt.Top + OkBt.Height + 495
End Sub
```

Q4. How to Make *.exe?

Ans. To make an executable from a project choose 'MakeMake project.exe from the 'File' menu. Then click once on the Make project.exe choose a default location to store your executable, you can also change some advanced options by clicking on the **Options..** tag before saving your exe

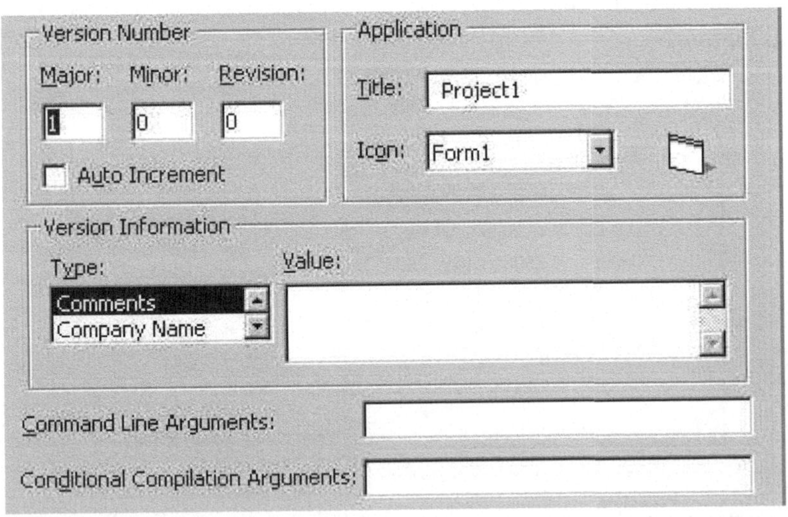

The above image will be displayed in the comment's value type some comments company name name etc... The Title tag represents the caption you will see if you press Control + Alt + Del. And the icon is the icon that will be available on the execute icon. As you can see it is quite simple to understand. All the comments, data and name appear when you click on the compiled (execute) exe and click properties.

Q5. How to Save visual basic project ?

Ans. Save your work to disk. Use the Windows Explorer or any desktop windows to check that all files have been saved. There should be one Visual Basic Project (.VBP) file and separate Form (.FRM) and Module (.BAS) files for each form and module used in the current project.

Q6. . List the various Button Properties.

 **Command Button & labels properties**

Ans.

Property	Description
Name	The name of the object so you can call it at runtime
BackColor	This specifies the command button's background color. Click the *BackColor's* palette down arrow to see a list of common Windows control colours, you must change this to the style property from 0 - standard to 1 – graphical
Cancel	Determines whether the command button gets a Click event if the user presses escape
Caption	Holds the text that appears on the command button.
Default	Determins if the command button responds to an enter keypress even if another control has the focus
Enable	Determines whether the command button is active. Often, you'll change the enable property at runtime with code to prevent the user pressing the button
Font	Produces a Font dialog box in which you can set the caption's font name, style and size.
Height	Positions the height of the object - can be used for down
Left	Positions the left control - can be used for right
MousePointer	If selected to an icon can change the picture of the mouse pointer over that object
Picture	Hold's the name of an icon graphic image so that it appears as a picture instead of a **Button** for this option to work the graphical tag must be set to 1
Style	This determins if the **Command Button** appears as a standard windows dialog box or a graphical image
Tab index	Specifies the order of the command button in tab order
Tab Stop	Whether the object can be tabbed to (this can be used in labels which have no other function)
Tool Tip Text	If the mouse is held over the object a brief description can be displayed (for example hold your mouse over one of the above pictures to see this happening
Visible	If you want the user to see the button/label select true other wise just press false
Width	Show the width of the object

Some Useful Concepts in VB

Q7. Define the term event ? How to use them ? Discuss with some examples.

Ans. The 'look' of a Visual Basic application is determined by what controls are used, but the 'feel' is determined by the events. An event is something which can happen to a control. For example, a user can click on a button, change a text box, or resize a form. As explained in Creating a Visual Basic Application, writing a program is made up of three events: 1) select suitable controls, 2) set the properties, and 3) write the code. It is at the code writing stage when it becomes important to choose appropriate events for each control. To do this double click on the control the event will be used for, or click on the  icon in the project window (usually top right of screen). A code window should now be displayed similar to the one shown below.

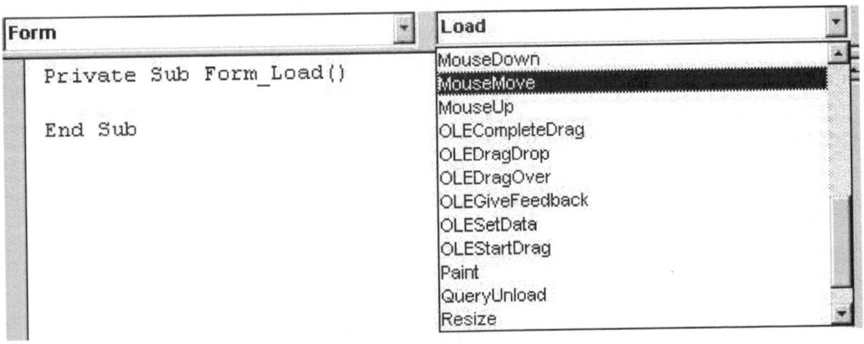

The left hand dropdown box provides a list of all controls used by the current form, the form itself, and a special section called General Declarations. The corresponding dropdown box on the right displays a list of all events applicable to the current control (as specified by the left hand dropdown box). Events displayed in bold signify that code has already been written for them, unbold events are unused. To demonstrate that different events can play a significant role in determining the feel of an application, a small example program will be written to add two numbers together and display the answer. The first solution to this problem will use the click event of a command button, while the second will the change event of two text boxes.

Click Event

Before any events can be coded it is necessary to design the interface from suitable controls. As shown in the screen shot below use: 2 text boxes to enter the numbers, a label for the '+' sign, a command button for the '=' sign, and another label for the answer.

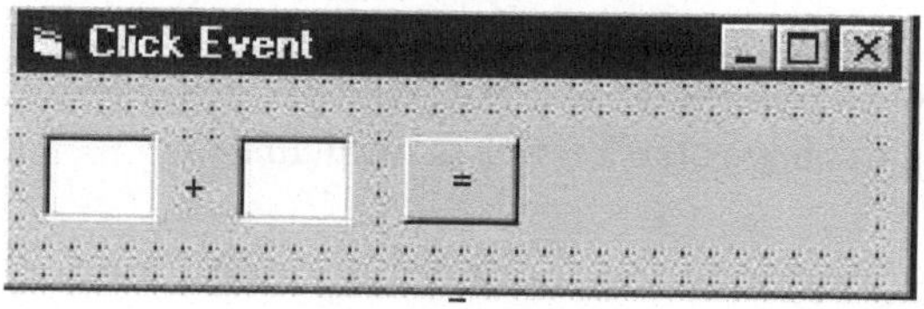

Making the click event is very simple just select the button with the mouse and double click visual basic will generate

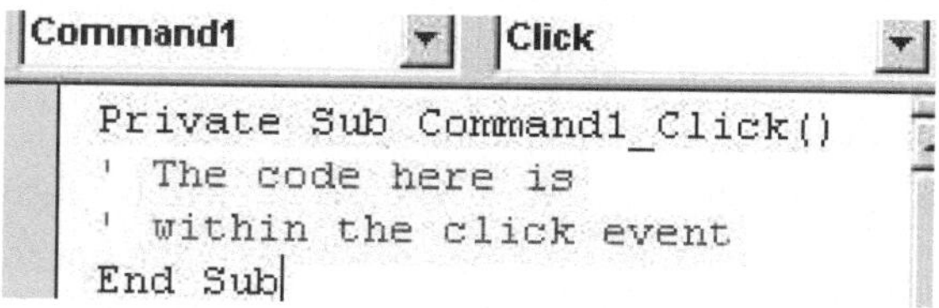

You can see on the top right there is a 'click' dropdown list this is known as a event handler.

Writing your own event

In the first example the user has to enter two numbers and then click on the equals button to produce an answer. However, the program can be changed so that the answer will be calculated every time either of the two numbers are changed without requiring an equals button.

To do this first remove the equals command button and replace it with a label with the caption set to '='. Now, bring up a code window and copy to the Windows clipboard the line **lblAnswer = Str$(Val(txtNumber1.Text) + Val(txtNumber2.Text))**. Using the left hand dropdown box select the first text box and then select the **Change** event from the right dropdown box. Then paste the code from the clipboard into the empty subroutine. Select the second text box and do the same. The same line is required twice because the two click events belong to two separate controls. The final code should look like:

Private Sub txtNumber1_Change()

```
label2.Caption = Str$(Val(text1.Text) + Val(text.Text))
End Sub

Private Sub txtNumber2_Change()
label2.Caption = Str$(Val(text1.Text) + Val(text2.Text))
End Sub
```

Run the program again, enter the two numbers and observe what happens. Each time a digit changes the answer is recalculated.

Note : There may be times when recalculating more advanced problems takes too long on each change and so requiring the user to enter all the data first and then click on an answer button might more appropriate.

Using the event GotFocus event

So far only one event has been used per control, however this does not have to be the case! Add a StatusBar control to the bottom of the form, bring up the code window using  , select the first text box (txtNumber1) from the left hand dropdown box, and then select the **`GotFocus`** event from the right hand dropdown box. Now some basic instructions can be written in the status bar so that when the cursor is in the text box (the text box has focus) the status bar reads "Enter the first number". After completing this change to the second text box and using the same GotFocus event change the statusbar text to "Enter a second number". The code to set the status bar can be seen below.

CheckBoxes

Option bars are used quite often in the windows environment as they can only have two outputs 0 and 1 these get used to process the form. In this example it will be used to change the some text from normal to bold or to italic.

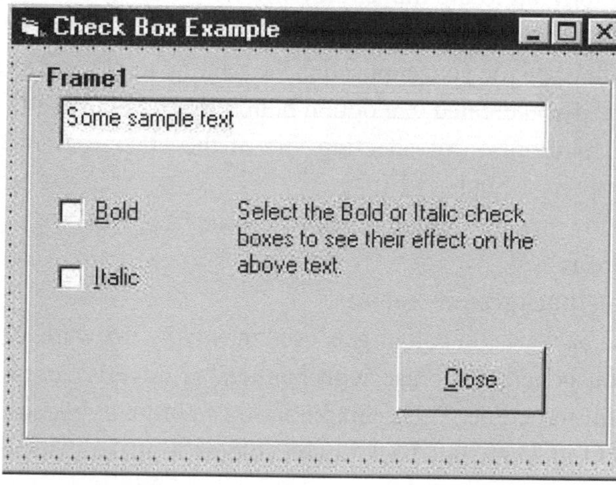


```
Private Sub chkBold_Click()
If chkBold.Value = 1 Then ' If checked.
txtDisplay.FontBold = True
Else ' If not checked.
txtDisplay.FontBold = False
End If
End Sub

Private Sub chkItalic_Click()
If chkItalic.Value = 1 Then ' If checked.
txtDisplay.FontItalic = True
Else ' If not checked.
txtDisplay.FontItalic = False
End If
End Sub
```

The checkboxes can be turned on at runtime by simply typing
name.value = 1 ' 1 On , 0 off

Note : If you create the frame first and then add the option buttons by single clicking on the toolbox and dragging the cross hair cursor on the frame to create the controls, they will be attached to the frame and will move with it if you decide to re-position the frame. Notice, however, that if you create the frame first and double click the screen controls, then drag them from the centre of the form on to the frame, they will not be attached to it and will be left behind when you try to move the frame.

Notice that when you run your application the same icon is loaded first (probably the clipboard, if you created that option button first). You can alter the option that has the focus first, by selecting one of the other option buttons and setting its property tabindex to 1.

Option Buttons

Changing the background colour

Changing the background colour gets used mostly by freeware, or the type of programs you generate for use with banners or adverts, anyway it might come in useful sometime. This example shows an ordinary picture of a smiley face then I put in some nice background colours to make it stand out more.

```
Private Sub Form_Load()
BackColor = QBColor(Rnd * 15)
ForeColor = QBColor(Rnd * 10)
Picture1.BackColor = QBColor(Rnd * 15)
Picture1.ForeColor = QBColor(Rnd * 10)
End Sub
```

List boxes

Note :

List boxes and combo boxes are used to supply a list of options to the user.

The toolbox icons representing these two controls are  for list box and  for combo box.

A list box is used when the user is to be presented with a fixed set of selections (i.e. a choice must be made only from the items displayed, there is no possibility of the user typing in an alternative).
Examples might be offering a list of the days in a week, the available modules in an elective catalogue, the holiday destinations available from a particular airport or the types of treatment offered by a beauty salon.

To create a list box, double click on the toolbox icon . Drag the resulting box into place on the form and size it according to the data it will hold. The left hand picture below shows a list box that has been created and sized on `Form1`. In the middle is the code that is required to load a selection of cars into the list. The data has been included in the procedure Sub Form_Load so that it appears when Form1 is loaded. Finally, the picture on the right shows what appears on the form when the application is run. Notice that vertical scroll bars are added automatically if the list box is not deep enough to display all the choices.

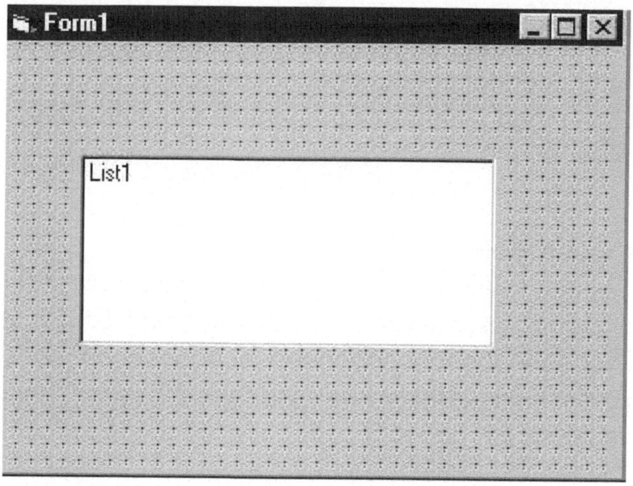

If you however add the following source code to this project

Add to a Lisbox

Private Sub Form_Load()
List1.AddItem "Monday"
List1.AddItem "Tuesday"
List1.AddItem "Wednesday"

List1.AddItem "Thursday"
List1.AddItem "Friday"
List1.AddItem "Saturday"
List1.AddItem "Sunday"
End Sub

The source code should look something like this :

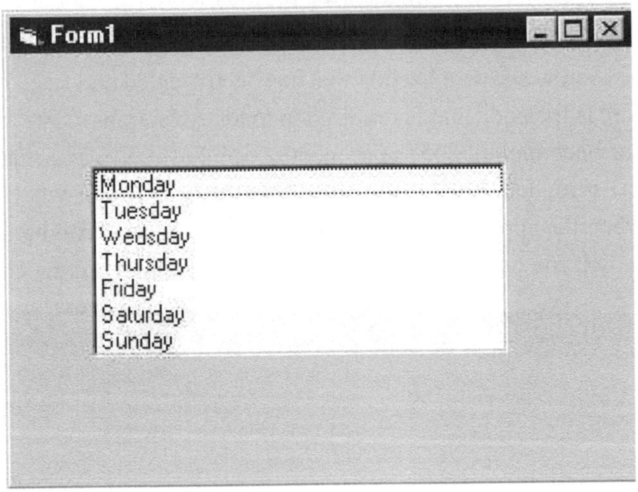

Removing & Advanced Options

Note: They appear in the order they were typed if you changed the properties window by changing sort order = true then they will go into alphabetical order. List items can be added and deleted all the list is counted as the order they are in so for example if you wanted to delete "Tuesday" you would type

list1.RemoveItem 1

And to add to the list in a particular order just add

list1.additem "My Day", 5

This will be added after Saturday.

And finally to clear the lisbox type

List1.clear This will completely clear the concept of the listbox.

Note: The property ListCount stores the number of items in a list, so list1.ListCount can be used to determine the number of items in list box list1. The property ListIndex gives the index of the currently selected list item. So the statement list1.RemoveItem List1. ListIndex removes the currently highlighted list item.

Adding an item can be accomplished very neatly using an input dialog box. Try this:

list1.AddItem InputBox("Enter a day", "Add a Day")

This will open a message box and prompt you for a new day to enter this will then be added to the list index at the bottom unless you specify where it should go.

Combo Boxes

Combo boxes are of three types (0,1 and 2), setting their properties/styles determines the type. Combo boxes (style 0 and 2) are a good choice if space is limited, because the full list is displayed as a drop down list, it does not occupy screen space until the down arrow is clicked.

Picture of combo box style 0

The user can either enter text in the edit field or select from the list of items by clicking on the (detached) down arrow to the right. The drop-down Combo box, list is viewed by clicking on the down arrow. This type of combo box does not have a down arrow because the list is displayed at all times. If there are more items then can be shown in the size of box you have drawn, vertical scroll bars are automatically added. As with previous type, users can enter text in the edit field.

Drop-down List box (Style=2)

It is slightly confusing to find this control under combo box. This control behaves like a regular list box except that the choices are not revealed until the down arrow is clicked. The user can select only from the choices given, there is no text entry facility.

Note: Combo boxes of style 0 and 2 cannot respond to double click events.

Q8. What are Msgboxes ?

Ans. Message boxes are used when you want to ask the user a question or display an error message(s) and advise the user. There are six types of message boxes here are their functions and what they do. Here is the listing of all the possible msgbox events

The Buttons displayed in a message here

Button Layout	Value	Short Description
VbOKonly	0	Displays the OK button.
VbOKCancel	1	Displays the ok and cancel button.
VbAbortRetryIgnore	2	Displays the Abort, Retry, Ignore
VbYesNoCancel	3	Displays Yes, No and Cancel button
VbYesNo	4	Displays the Yes / No button
VbRetryCancel	5	Displays the retry and Cancel buttons.

The Icons displayed in the message box are here

Icon on message	Value	Short Description
vbCritical	16	Displays critical message icon
vbQuestion	32	Displays question icon
vbExclamation	48	Displays exclamation icon
vbInformation	64	Displays information icon

The Default button displayed in a message form

Default Button	Value	Short Description
vbDefaultButton1	0	Button 1 is default
vbDefaultButton2	256	Button 2 is default
vbDefaultButton3	512	Button 3 is default

Msgbox Return Value

Return Value	Value	Short Description
vbOk	1	The User Clicked OK
vbCancel	2	The User Clicked Cancel
vbAbort	3	The User Clicked Abort
vbRetry	4	The User Clicked Retry
vbIgnore	5	The User Clicked Ignore
VbYes	6	The User Clicked Yes
VbNo	7	The User Clicked No

The syntax for use of the message box in Msgbox "TEXT", VALUE, "TITLE" If you want to use two or more tables just add the values together. Therefore to print a message box to say "The Device was not Found!" OK & Explanation :

Source code 1

```
Private Sub Form_Load()
MsgBox "The Device was not Found!", 48, "Header"
End Sub
```

Source code 2

```
Private Sub Form_Load()
MsgBox "The Device was not found!", vbExclamation, "Header"
End Sub
```

You should get the picture shown below whatever source code you used.

This is a basic msgbox which in this case has not been processed in any way. The following Source code displays a msgbox that ask you for specific text. For example lets make a password program out of this message box.

```
Private Sub Form_Load()
lngBefore = Timer
Do
strAns = InputBox("What is the password Password is Example", "Password
Required")
Loop Until Val(strAns) = Example
lngAfter = Timer
msgbox "Correct Password", vbInformation
End Sub
```

Once you copy and paste the source code you should get prompted for a password in a different type of msgbox as it includes text. From looking at this example you should be able to see how the loop function works to generate and then check the value. All of the Return Values work in the same way to return an object input.

Q9. Discuss the way for Opening & Retrieving information from files.

Ans. When applications are loaded they normal get some setting out of the registry or file this section will show you how to retrieve 1 string out of a file.

```
Private Sub Form_Load()
Dim F As Integer, password As String
F = FreeFile
Open App.Path & "\gullybaba.txt" For Input As F
Input #F, password
Close #F

End Sub
```

As you can see from this source code the password is previously declared as a string. After this is done be sure to close the file otherwise next time you want to store or read the file the computer will think it is being used by another application and windows will not let you do anything with it. So as you can see it is **Very Important** to close the file

Q10. Write an introduction to the usages of Access databases. Discuss about various components / objects used in the process of database handling in VB.

Ans. There are many ways to work with databases in Visual Basic, and I would think you have at least glanced at the Data control. I will not even mention the Data control further in this text, since it is so easy to use and too limited to be interesting for a professional developer. (Ok, there are some exceptions to this.)

What I will teach you to use in this text is DAO (Data Access Objects). You will get familiar with opening a database and retrieving/adding/deleting/updating records from tables. I will only use an Access Database (*.mdb) in my examples, since this is the most used DBMS (DataBase Management System) for smaller applications made in Visual Basic. We will at the end of this lesson have made a simple, yet functional, phone book application.

This text requires some knowledge of the Visual Basic programming language and you should be familiar with the Visual Basic IDE (Integrated Development Environment).

Database Object

The first thing you must do in your application is to open a database where your tables are stored. You need to declare a variable to hold your database in order to do this. This is done with:

```
Dim dbMyDB As Database
```

This gives you a variable/object that can hold a reference to your database. To open a simple Access database named "MyDatabase.mdb", do this:

Set dbMyDB = OpenDatabase("MyDatabase.mdb")

You should really specify the complete path to the db, but if your current directory is the directory where the database is situated, this will work.

So, now you have opened a database. This won't give you any data. What you need to do is open a table in the database. You're not limited to open a single table; sometimes you have two or more tables that are related to each other and linked together with foreign keys, and there are ways to handle this to. Here in "Visual Basic - Database Primer" first learn how to open a single table.

RecordSet Object

Visual Basic uses an object called RecordSet to hold your table. To declare such an object and to open the table, do this:

Dim rsMyRS As RecordSet

Set rsMyRS = dbMyDB.OpenRecordSet("MyTable", dbOpenDynaset)

A RecordSet object is declared and used the Database object's OpenRecordSet method to open a table of type Dynaset. You can open a RecordSet in several modes. The Dynaset mode is the mode I use mostly. It gives you a RecordSet that you can add, delete and modify records in.

Accessing records

Now that we have opened a table (referred to as RecordSet from now on) we want to access the records in it. The RecordSet object allows us to move in it by using the methods MoveFirst, MoveNext, MovePrevious, MoveLast (among others). I will use some of these to fill up a list box with the records of our RecordSet.

To get this example to work, make a database (with Access) called "MyDatabase.mdb" with the table "MyTable" in it. This table should have the fields "ID" of type "Counter" that you set to be the primary key, the field "Name" of type Text and a field "Phone" of type Text. Add some records to it. Put a list box on a form and call it "lstRecords".

Dim dbMyDB As Database

Dim rsMyRS As RecordSet

Private Sub Form_Load()

```
Set dbMyDB = OpenDatabase("MyDatabase.mdb")
Set rsMyRS = dbMyDB.OpenRecordSet("MyTable", dbOpenDynaset)
If Not rsMyRS.EOF Then rsMyRS.MoveFirst
Do While Not rsMyRS.EOF
        lstRecords.AddItem rsMyRS!Name
        lstRecords.ItemData(lstRecords.NewIndex) = rsMyRS!ID
        rsMyRS.MoveNext
Loop

End Sub
```

This will make the list box fill up with your records when the form loads. I have introduced some new concepts with this example. We have all ready covered the first part where we open the table. The line that says If Not rsMyRS.EOF Then rsMyRS.MoveFirst tells the program to move to the first record in case there are any records at all. The EOF is a Boolean property that is true if the current record is the last. It is also true if there are no records in the RecordSet.

Then we make the program add the "Name" field of all records to the list box by adding the current records field "Name" and moving to the next record. You ask for a field of a RecordSet by putting a ! between the name of the RecordSet object and the name of the field. The while loop checks to see if there are more records to add.

Searching the RecordSet

You might have wondered why I put the value of the field "ID" in the list box's ItemData property. I did this so that we would know the primary key for all the records in order to search for a record.

Put a text box somewhere on the form and call it "txtPhone". Then copy the following code to the project.

```
Private Sub lstRecords_Click()

rsMyRS.FindFirst "ID=" & Str(lstRecords.ItemData(lstRecords.ListIndex))
txtPhone.Text = rsMyRS!Phone

End Sub
```

This will display the phone number of the selected person when clicking in the list box. It uses the FindFirst method of the RecordSet object. This takes a string parameter that is like what is after WHERE in a SQL expression. You state the field that you want to search in (here "ID"), then the evaluation criteria (here "=") and last the value to search for (here the ItemData of the selected item in the list box).

So what we did was to search for the record with the "ID" field value that was the same as the ItemData property of the selected item in the list box. Then we show the value of the "Phone" field in the text box.

Updating the Database

You will probably want to be able to update some value of some field when doing database programming. This is done with Edit and Update. We will try to change the value of the "Phone" field by editing the text in the text box and clicking a button.

Put a command button on the form and name it "cmdUpdate". Then copy the following code to the project.

```
Private Sub cmdUpdate_Click()

rsMyRS.Edit
rsMyRS!Phone = txtPhone.Text
rsMyRS.Update

End Sub
```

Could it be that simple? Yes. This changes the phonenumber of our selected person. Or to put it technically: This changes the value of the "Phone" field of our current record. Imagine the current record being a set of boxes, with a field in each box. The Edit method takes the lid off all of the boxes and Update puts them back on. When we write rsMyRS!Phone = txtPhone.Text we replace the content of the "Phone" box with the content in the text box.

Deleting and Adding records

Deleting records couldn't be simpler. To delete the current record you just invoke the Delete method of the RecordSet object. We will put this feature in our little project. Make one more command button named "cmdDelete" and the following code will do the work of deleting our currently selected person.

```
Private Sub cmdDelete_Click()

rsMyRS.Delete
```

```
lstRecords.RemoveItem lstRecords.ListIndex

End Sub
```

I won't even bother to explain that in greater detail =). The first statement deletes the record and the second removes the list box entry.

Adding

Adding records is much like updating, except you use AddNew instead of Edit. Let's add one more command button to our application. Let's call it...errh...let me see...yea! "cmdNew" =). Here is the code that adds a new record.

```
Private Sub cmdNew_Click()

rsMyRS.AddNew
rsMyRS!Name = "A New Person"
lstRecords.AddItem rsMyRS!Name
lstRecords.ItemData(lstRecords.NewIndex) = rsMyRS!ID
rsMyRS!Phone = "Person's Phone Number"
rsMyRS.Update

End Sub
```

I will use the box analogy to explain this. The AddNew method takes a set of new boxes and adds them to our RecordSet. We then put some new values in them and close the lids with Update. As you can see we never stated any value for "ID", but as you remember, this is a field of type "Counter" which automatically gets a unique value. The code also adds this new record to the list box so that we will be able to change the phone number of this person.

Chapter - 6

Database With VB

Introduction : VB allows you to access and manipulate data in databases. It also allows you to manage databases, Objects and Structures. It includes a number of features that make database access relatively simple like:

• Close attachment with the Microsoft Access Database Program.

• Data Control to access the display database information within other controls.

• Capability to work with ODBC and SQL drivers in order to access and manage data in relational databases.

Visual Basic includes the Microsoft Jet Database Engine with powers Microsoft Access. It allows you to display, edit and update information from many types of databases.

In Visual Basic standard edition, you can use the Data control to access information in existing databases.

In Visual Basic professional edition, you can also create or modify databases using the Data Access Objects programming interface.

Using Data Control: You can use the data control to create applications that display, edit and update information from many types of existing databases, including Microsoft Access, Btrieve, dBase, Microsoft Foxpro®, and Paradox. You can also use it to access Microsoft Excel, Lotus 1-2-3, and standard ASCII text files as if they were true databases. In addition, the data control allows you to access and manipulate remote Open Database Connectivity (ODBC) databases such as Microsoft SQL Server and Oracle.

The data control implements data access by using the Microsoft Jet database engine, the same database engine that powers Microsoft Access. This technology gives you seamless access to many standard database formats and allows you to create data aware applications without writing any code.

You can use the data control to create simple database applications without writing any code at all. You can also use it together with Visual Basic code to create full featured applications that give you a high degree of programming control over the behavior of your application's data. This topic will consider the simple no-code approach. Succeeding topics will present more complex programming examples.

The data control can perform the following tasks without the use of code :

• Connect to a local or remote database.

• Open a specified database table or define a set of records based on a Structured Query Language (SQL) query of the tables in that database.

• Pass data fields to bound controls, where you can display and change the values.

• Add new records or update a database based on any changes you make to data displayed in the bound controls.

• Trap errors that occur as data is accessed.

• Close the database.

To create a database application, you add the data control to your forms just as you would any other Visual Basic control. You can have as many data controls on your form as you need. As a rule, you will use one data control for each database table that you need to manipulate.

To create a simple database application, follow these steps :

1. Add the **Data** control to a form.
2. Set its properties to indicate the database and table from which you want to get information.
3. Add bound controls (such as text boxes, list boxes, and other controls that you "bind" to the data control).
4. Set the properties of the bound controls to indicate the data source and data field to be displayed.
When you run the application, these bound control automatically display fields from the current record in the database.

Data Control Properties : Like all Visual Basic controls, the data control has some properties that must be set in the properties window at design time. Many of these can also be set at run time in Visual Basic code.
To use data control, at a minimum you must set the DatabaseName and RecordSource properties. Once you have set the DatabaseName property, Visual Basic will retrieve the names of all tables and available queries in the database and display them in the dropdown list of the RecordSource property.
If you want to open an external database (Foxpro, Btrieve, Paradox, dBase, Microsoft Excel, Lotus 1-2-3, Text or ODBC), you must also set the Connect property using the Properties Window.
Once you choose a table or query from the list, you will be able to use the Properties window to select a valid DataField property setting on each of your bound controls.
You can also set or change the data control and bound control properties at run time. Once the correct properties are set, you can use the data control's Refresh method to reopen the database (if necessary) and rebuild the recordset with the new property settings.
The following procedure gives you a brief overview of how to use the data control in a Visual Basic application. The example uses the Biblio.mdb sample database supplied with Visual Basic.
Tutorial : Using Data Control

• **To use the data control in an application**
1. Select the **data** control in the Toolbox, and draw a data control on a form.
Data Control:

The data control button looks like this:

Figure: Data Control on a Form

Database Using Visual Basic Data Access Object

Objective:

- Learn the use of data access object
- Accessing data into an application using data access object.

Introduction: This chapter includes the Microsoft Jet database engine and its programming model, Data Access Objects (DAO). It presents the basic concepts of relational database design and shows how to create, maintain and modify databases using the data definition language (DDL) methods of DAO. It explains how to use DAO to define database tables, fields and indexes and how to create relations between tables. Also included are techniques for modifying database structure and maintaining existing databases.

The Microsoft Jet Database Engine: Visual Basic provides data access capability based on the Microsoft Jet database engine, the same database engine that powers Microsoft Access. The Jet engine handles the mechanics of storing, retrieving and updating data and provides you with the powerful DAO object-oriented programming interface.

Visual Basic version 5.0 comes with version 3.5 of the Microsoft Jet database engine, a 32-bit only engine. Because it is backward compatible with earlier versions of the Jet database engine, your 16-bit applications written in earlier versions of Visual Basic can easily be upgraded to take advantage of the additional features and performance improvements in version 5.0.

A Visual Basic database application has three parts, as shown below.

User Interface and Application Code: The user interface is what the user sees and interacts with. It contains forms that display the data and enable the user to view and update it. Driving these forms is you're application's Visual Basic code, including data access objects and methods to request database services like adding or deleting records or performing queries.

As the above illustration shows, these requests for services are not directed to the physical database file, but to the Jet database engine, which performs the requested operations on the data store and returns the desired results to the application.

The Database Engine: The Jet database engine is contained in a set of dynamic link library (DLL) files that are linked to your Visual Basic program at run time. It translates the application's requests into physical considerations on the .mdb file or other data source. It is what actually reads, writes and modifies the database and handles all the housekeeping chores like indexing, locking, security and referential integrity. It also contains a query processor that accepts your Structured Query Language (SQL) queries and acts on them to carry out the desired database operations, and a results processor to manage the results returned by queries.

The Data Store: The Data store is the file or files containing the database tables themselves. For native Visual Basic or Microsoft Access databases, this is an .mdb file. For different databases it might be a directory containing files with .dbf or other extensions. Or, your application might access data stored in several different database files and formats. In any case, the data store is essentially passive. It contains the data, but doesn't *do* anything to or with it. That is the job of the database engine.

The three components can be divided in many ways. All three parts can be present on one computer in a single-user application. Or, they can be located on different computers connected over a network. For example, the data store might reside on a central file server, and the user interface (the "application program") on several workstations, giving many users access to the same data.

Remote vs. Client/Server(Optional): An important distinction in database applications where the data is stored on a different machine from the application program, is between a *remote* database and a *client/server* database. The difference is illustrated below.

In a client/server system, the database engine is located on a central server, along with the data store. The engine can service many "client" applications simultaneously, manipulating the data store and returning the requested records to each local application. In a remote system, the database engine is on the same computer as the user application, with only the data store residing on a remote machine.

The Jet database engine is not a client/server engine. It is a local database engine residing in DLL files that are dynamically linked to your Visual Basic program at run time. If there are many copies of your program on different workstations, each will have its own local copy of the Jet database engine, even though they may be accessing a single remote database.

To create a new database:

1. Use the Dim statement to create new object variable for each object in your database. In addition to the DBEngine and default Workspace objects that make up the working environment, you will need:

- One Database object
- One TableDef object for each table
- One Field object for each field in such table
- One Index object for each index in each table

For example, to create object variables for the Biblio.mdb database, you could use the following code :

```
Dim DBMine As Database, WSMine As Workspace
Dim AaTD as TableDef, TitTd As TableDef, _
PubTd as TableDef
Dim AuFlds (2) As Field, TitFlds as Field
Dim AuIdx As Index
```

2. Use the CreateDatabase method of the Workspace object to create the new database. In this example, the method uses minimum two arguments: one to specify the database name, and one to specify the locale:

```
Set WsMine = DBEngine, Workspaces (0)
Set DBMine = WsMine.CreateDatabase _
("C:\VB\Biblio.mdb", dbLangGeneral, dbVersion30)
```

Note that the constant dbVersion specifies a Jet version 3.0 database. If you use the dbVersion30 constant to create a version 3.0 database, only 32-bit applications using the Jet version 3.0 engine or higher will be able to access it.

3. Use the CreateTableDef method of the database object to create new TableDef objects for each table in the database, as follows:

Set TitTd = DBMine.CreateTableDef ("Titles")
Set AaTd = DBMine.CreateTableDef ("Authors")
Set PubTd = DBMine.CreateTableDef ("Publishers")

4. Use the CreateField method of the TableDef object to create new field objects for each field in the table, and to set properties of each field to define the field's size, data type and other needed attributes. For example, the following code creates the Author's table in the Biblio.mdb database:

/Set AuFlds (0) = AaTd.CreateField ("Au_ID", dbLong)
' Make it a counter field.
Auflds (0).Attributes = dbAutoIncrField
Set AuFlds (1) = AaTd.CreateField ("Author", dbText)
AuFlds (1).Size = 50
Set TitFlds = TitTd.CreateField ("Au_Id", dbLong)

5. Use the Append method to add each field to its table and each table to the database, as shown in the following code:

AaTd.Fields.Append Auflds (0)
AaTd.Fields.Append Auflds (1)
DBMine.TableDefs.Append AaTd

Note : In this example, a different variable is used for each data access object, for clarity. In practice, you can reuse the variables to simplify your code. For example, you can use the Dim statement to declare a single TableDef variable, use CreateTableDef to assign a new TableDef object to it, and append it to the Database. Once it is appended, you can use the same TableDef variable to create and append each new TableDef.

You add indexes to the TableDef by creating them with the CreateIndex method. In order to specify which fields are to be indexed, you create new field objects with the CreateField method of the Index object.

To add an index to a database table:

1. Create indexes for each table using the CreateIndex method of the TableDef object, and set their properties:

Set AuIdx = AaTd.CreateIndex ("Author ID")
AuIdx.Primary = True
AuIdx.Unique = True

2. Create fields for each index object using the CreateField method of the

Index object:

Set NewFld = AuIdx.CreateField ("Au_ID")

3. Append the field to the index and index to the TableDef object:

AuIdx.Fields.Append NewFld

AaTd.Indexes.Append AuIdx

Note: Fields created with the CreateField method of the Index object are not added to the TableDef. Instead, they are needed to the Index object, and given the Name property as the TableDef field that are to index. You do not specify Type and Size properties on fields of the Index object.

Chapter – 7

Previous Year Important Question Solutions

Q1. 'Description: A basic example of creating a addressbook 'using a Microsoft Access 2000 database.

Ans.

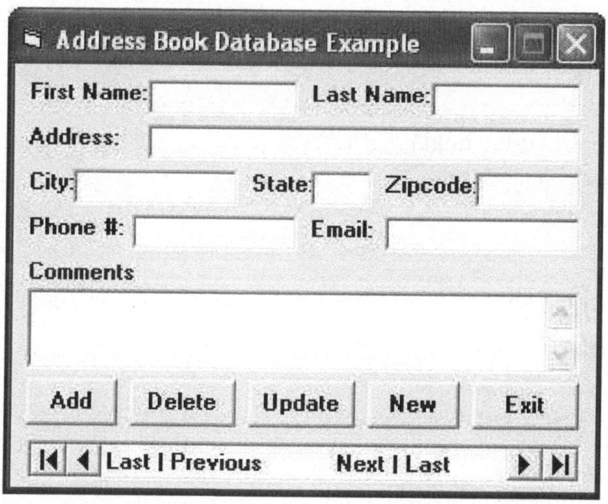

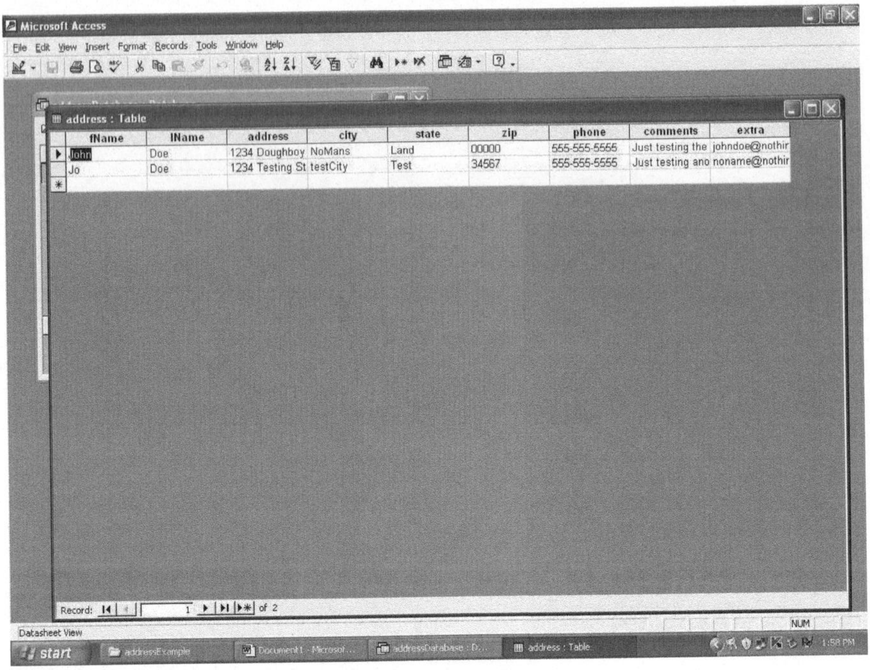


```
Private Sub Command2_Click()
databar.Recordset.Delete
databar.Recordset.MovePrevious
End Sub

Private Sub Command3_Click()
databar.Recordset.Edit
End Sub

Private Sub cmdAdd_Click()
    databar.Recordset.AddNew
End Sub

Private Sub cmdExit_Click()
   Unload Me
    End
End Sub

Private Sub cmdNew_Click()
```

```
    databar.Recordset.AddNew
End Sub
Private Sub cmdUpdate_Click()
    databar.UpdateRecord
End Sub

Private Sub txtAddress_GotFocus()
    txtAddress.SelStart = 0
    txtAddress.SelLength = Len(txtAddress.Text)
End Sub

Private Sub txtCity_GotFocus()
    txtCity.SelStart = 0
    txtCity.SelLength = Len(txtCity.Text)
End Sub

Private Sub txtComments_GotFocus()
    txtComments.SelStart = 0
    txtComments.SelLength = Len(txtComments.Text)
End Sub

Private Sub txtEmail_GotFocus()
    txtEmail.SelStart = 0
    txtEmail.SelLength = Len(txtEmail.Text)
End Sub

Private Sub txtFirst_GotFocus()
    txtFirst.SelStart = 0
    txtFirst.SelLength = Len(txtFirst.Text)
End Sub

Private Sub txtLast_GotFocus()
    txtLast.SelStart = 0
    txtLast.SelLength = Len(txtLast.Text)
End Sub
```

```
Private Sub txtPhone_GotFocus()
   txtPhone.SelStart = 0
   txtPhone.SelLength = Len(txtPhone.Text)
End Sub

Private Sub txtState_GotFocus()
   txtState.SelStart = 0
   txtState.SelLength = Len(txtState.Text)
End Sub

Private Sub txtZip_GotFocus()
   txtZip.SelStart = 0
   txtZip.SelLength = Len(txtZip.Text)
End Sub
```

Q2. Write a VB program to accept 2 given strings from the user and count the number of times the second string appears in the first string. Design and display a splash screen as your program loads. [June 2003, Set-3]

Ans. This problem is divided into two parts:

1. Provide a Splash screen

2. Provide a Form, which find the occurrences of a string from another string.

1. Provide a Splash screen:

- Add a Form to project and name it frmSplash
- Design the form as given in screen layout.

```
Private Sub Form_Load( )
lblVersion.Caption = "Version" & App.Major & "." & App.Minor & "."
App.Revision
lblProductName.Caption = App.Title
End Sub
```

2. Provide a Form, which find the occurrences of a string from another string.

This Form is design to find the occurrences of String 2 from String 1. String Library function **INSTR** is used to find the occurrence of one string from another string.

INSTR:

Syntax: Instr (Start as integer, String1, String2, flag as integer) As integer

This function returns the position in String1, where string2 is matched. The function starts scanning from the position start.
flag = 0 for binary comparison
flag = 1 for textual comparison
This form has used following components to solve the above problem.

Object	**Description**	**Name**	**Properties**
Label	show "String Occurrence"	Label1	Name: Label1 Caption: "String Occurrence"
Label	Show "Input String"	Label2	Name: Label2 Caption: Input String
Label	Show "String to be searched"	Label3	Name: Label3 Caption: String to be searched
Label	Show "No. of Occurrence"	Label4	Name: Label4 Caption: No. of Occurrence
Command Button	Provide an Event, at which no. of occurrences from string 1 will be calculated	cmd_find	Name: cmd_find Caption: &Find

CODE:

```
Private Sub cmd_Find_Click( )
Dim pos, p_pos, cnt As Integer
p_pos = 1
```

```
pos=1
cnt = 0

Do
pos = InStr(p_pos,txtin,txt_search, vbTextCompare)
p_pos = p_pos + pos
If pos < > 0 Then cnt = cnt + 1
Loop While pos < > 0

txt_occ.Text = cnt
End Sub

'As there is no Form set as startup. Application start execution from Sub
' Main( ), which is as below:
Public tMainForm As frmMain

Sub Main( )
frmSplash.Show
frmSplash.Refresh
Set fMainForm = New frmMain
Load fMainForm
Unload frmSplash
fMainForm.Show
End Sub
```

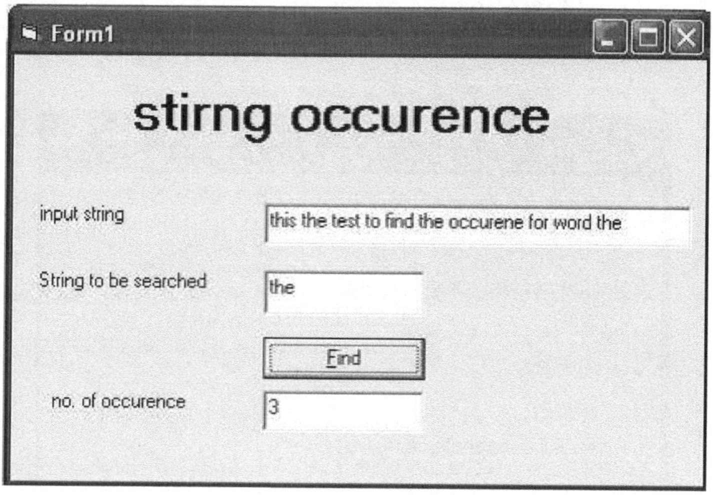

Q3. Write a VB program to accept 2 given strings, concatenate them and find the length of the resultant string.

[June 2003, Set-4]

Ans. Form1 is designed to solve above problem.

• **Contains:** 4 textboxes, 1 command button

Property setting for these components (Except Labels) are as:

Object	Field	Name	Properties
Textbox	To get string1	Text1	Font: mssanssarif-14 Text: null
Textbox	To get string2	Text2	Font: mssanssarif-14 Text: null
Textbox	To print concatenated string	Text3	Font: mssanssarif-14 Text: null
Textbox	To print length of resultant string	Text4	Font: mssanssarif-14 Text: null
Command button	To get concatenated string and its length	Command1	Font: mssanssarif-14 Caption: Concatenate

SOURCE CODE:

```
Private Sub Command1_Click( )
```

```
Text3.Text = Text1.Text & Text2.Text
Text4.Text = Len(Text3.Text)
End Sub
```

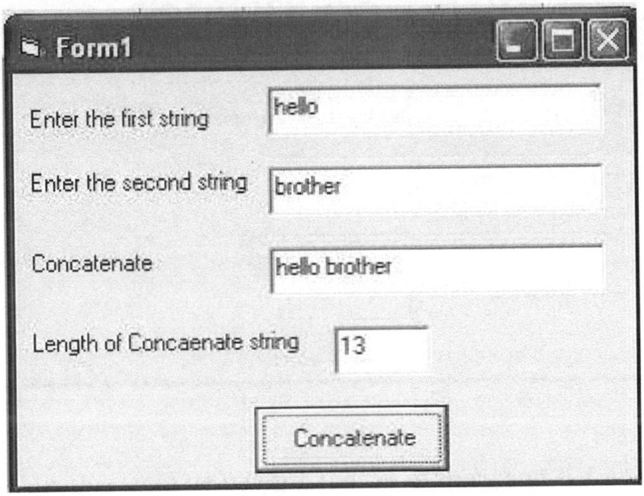

A space is present between hello and brother because of a space is used after hello

Q4. Write a VB program in which function accepts the integer value from user and displays the diamond shape according to the User Input.

[June 2004, Set-1]

e.g. Input = 5

```
  *
 ***
*****
 ***
  *
```

Ans. Form frmDiamond is design to take values from the user and displays the diamond shape according to the User input.

frmDiamond has one command button object to display the diamond shape to user and one text box to take user input.

Object	Description	Name	Properties
Form	Contain application that display the diamond shape according to the user input	frmDiamond	**Name:** frmDiamond **Caption:** Diamond Display **Height:** 3600 **Width:** 4800
Text	Get the input from the user	txtInput	**Name:** txtInput **Text:**
List	To show the diamond shape	1stDisplay	**Name:** 1stDisplay **Text:**
Command	To display the diamond shape	cmdDisplay	**Name:** cmdDisplay **Caption:** Display

Source Code

```
Private Sub cmd_Display_Click( )
Dim i
Dim j
Dim NumLines, str

NumLines = Cint(txtInput)
1stDisplay.Clear

For i = 0 To NumLines/2
For j = i To NumLines/2 + 1
str = str & " "
Next

For j = 0 To i Step 1
str = str & "* "
Next

Display.AddItem (str)
str = " "
Next

For i = 1 To NumLines/2
```

```
For j = 0 To i + 1
str = str & " "
Next

For j = i To NumLines/2
str = str & "* "
Next

Display.AddItem (str)
str = " "
Next

End Sub
```

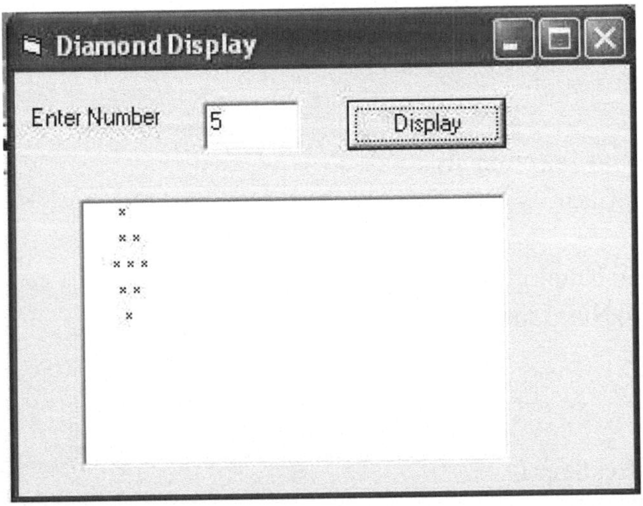

Q5. Create a VB program to calculate the income tax. User will put his Annual Income in the box and by clocking on "Income tax" button, message box will show his income tax according to the following rule:

[June 2004, Set-1]

0	-	Rs.50000	→	No tax
Rs.50000	-	Rs.6000	→	10% of Annual Income
Rs.60000	-	Rs.150000	→	20% of Annual Income
More than Rs.150000			→	30% of Annual Income

Ans. Form frmIncomeTax is design to take annual income from the user and displays the income tax on clicking "Income tax" button.

frmIncomeTax has one command button object to calculate the income tax and two text box objects – one text box to take annual income from user and second text box to display the income tax to the user.

Object	Description	Name	Properties
Form	Contain application that takes annual income from the user and displays the income tax	frmIncomeTax	**Name:** frmIncomeTax **Caption:** Income Tax Calculation **Height:** 1845 **Width:** 4170
Text	Get the annual income from the user	TxtAnnualIncome	**Name:** txtAnnualIncome **Text:**
List	To show the income text	1stDisplay	**Name:** 1stDisplay **Text:**
Command	To display the income text	cmdIncomeTax	**Name:** cmdIncomeTax **Caption:** Income Tax

Source Code

```
Private Sub cmdIncomeTax_Click( )
Dim AI As Double
AI = Val(txtAnnualIncome)
If AI > 0 And AI < 50000 Then
txtIncomeTax = "No tax"
Else
If AI > 50000 And AI < 60000 Then
txtIncomeTax = AI * 0.1
Else
```

```
If AI > 60000 And AI < 150000 Then
txtIncomeTax = AI * 0.2
Else
If AI > 150000 Then
txtIncomeTax = AI * 0.3
End If
End If
End If
End If
```

End Sub

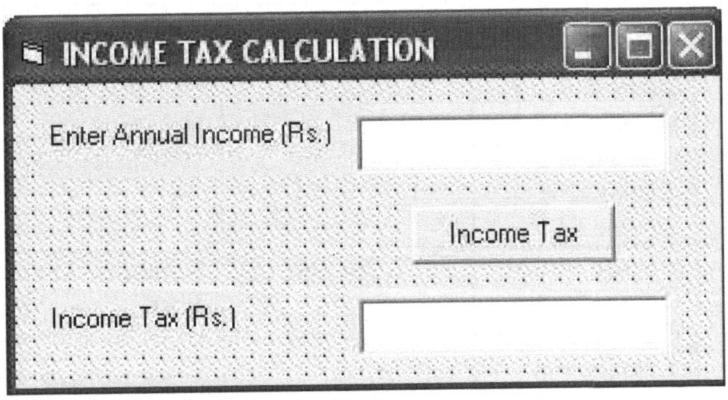

Q6. Write a program in VB to convert the Celsius to Fahrenheit and Fahrenheit to Celsius. Provide two buttons and one text box. One button converts Fahrenheit to Celsius and the other convert Celsius to Fahrenheit. Use the formula:

[June 2004, Set-2]

Celsius = (5/9) * (Fahrenheit – 32)

Ans. Form frmIncomeTax is design to take annual income from the user and displays the income tax on clicking "Income tax" button.

frmIncomeTax has one command button object to calculate the income tax and two text box objects – one text box to take annual income from user and second text box to display the income tax to the user.

Object	Description	Name	Properties
Form	Contain application that takes annual income from the user and displays the income tax	frmTemperature	**Name:** frmTemperature **Caption:** Temperature Calculation **Height:** 2175 **Width:** 4260
Text	Get the temperature from the user	txtInput	**Name:** txtInput **Text:**
Text	To show the conversion temperature	txtResult	**Name:** txtResult **Text:**
Command	To do conversion the temperature in to Celsius	cmdCelsius	**Name:** cmdCelsius **Caption:** Celsius
Command	To do conversion the temperature in to Fahrenheit	cmdFahrenheit	**Name:** cmdFahrenheit **Caption:** Fahrenheit

Source Code

```
Dim c, f As Double
Private Sub cmdCelsius_Click( )
f = Val(txtInput)
c = Round((5/9) * (f – 32), 2)
txtResult = str(f ) & "degree Fahrenheit = " & str(c) & "degree Celsius"
End Sub

Private Sub cmdFahrenheit_Click( )
c = Val(txtInput)
f = Round((c* 1.8) + 32, 2)
txtResult = str(c) & "degree Celsius = " & (f ) & "degree Fahrenheit"
End Sub
```

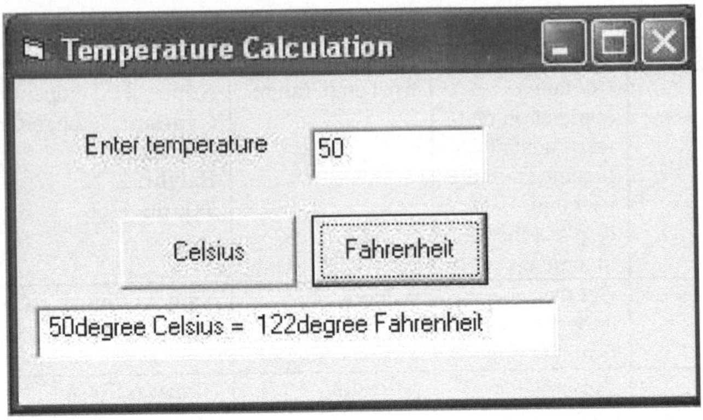

Q7. Write a program in VB for Encryption and Decryption using the simple logic given below:

A ↔ 1

B ↔ 2

...

...

Z ↔ 26

In a text box, user types a message in English. On pressing Encrypt button, program will convert that message into integer form and on pressing Decrypt, button it will convert the integer values into the character (English) pattern.

[June 2004, Set-2]

Ans. Form frmEncryption is design to take message from the user and displays the encrypted message on clicking "Encrypt" button.

frmEncryption has a command button object to Encrypt the user message and two text box objects – one text box to take user message and second text box to display the encrypted message to the user.

Object	Description	Name	Properties
Form	Contain application that encrypt the user message	frmEncryption	**Name:** frmEncryption **Caption:** Encryption **Height:** 1950 **Width:** 4800
Text	Get the message from the user	txtInput	**Name:** txtInput **Text:**
Text	To show the encrypted message to the user	txtEncrypt	**Name:** txtEncrypt **Text:**
Command	To do encryption of the user message	cmdEncrypt	**Name:** cmdEncrypt **Caption:** Encrypt

Source Code

```
Dim iCounter As Integer
Dim ch As String

Private Sub cmdEncrypt_Click()

For iCounter = 1 To Len(txtInput)
ch = Mid(txtInput, iCounter, 1)
ch = UCase(ch)
j = Asc(ch) - 64
txtEncrypt.Text = Str(j)
Next
End Sub
```

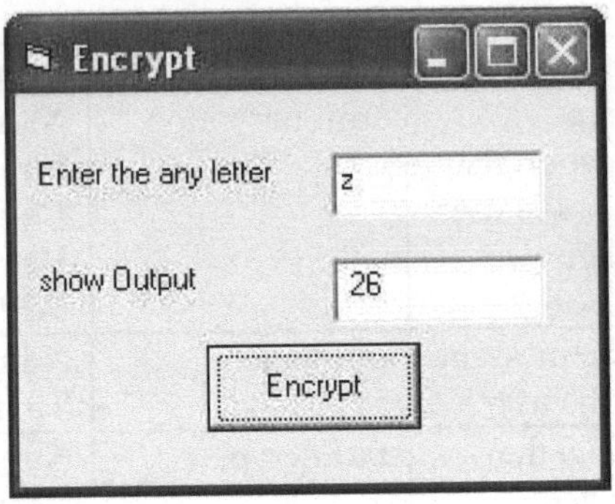

Q8. Write a program in VB, which calculates and displays the prime numbers between the given ranges of integers by the user.

[June 2004, Set-3]

Ans. Form frmPrimeNumber is design to take starting range and ending range from the user and displays the prime numbers between given range. frmPrimeNumber has a command button object to Encrypt the user message and two text box objects – one text box to take user message and second text box to display the encrypted message to the user.

Object	Description	Name	Properties
Form	Contain application that encrypt the user message	frmPrimeNumber	**Name:** frmPrimeNumber **Caption:** Display Prime Number **Height:** 1695 **Width:** 4470
Text	Get the starting range from the user	txtStartNo	**Name:** txtStartNo **Text:**
Text	Get the ending range from the user	txtEndNo	**Name:** txtEndNo **Text:**
Text	To show the prime numbers to the user	txtprime	**Name:** txtprime **Text:**
Command	To do calculate the prime number and display it	cmdDisplay	**Name:** cmdDisplay **Caption:** Display Prime Numbers

Source Code

```
Private Sub cmdDisplay_Click()
Dim iCounter As Integer
```

```
Dim Stranger As Integer
Dim Endrange As Integer
Dim jCounter As Integer
Dim counter As Integer

Strange = CInt(txtStartNo)
Endrange = CInt(txtEndNo)

For iCounter = Strange To Endrange
counter = 0
For jCounter = 2 To iCounter - 1
If iCounter Mod jCounter = 0 Then
counter = counter + 1
End If
Next

If counter = 0 Then
txtprime = txtprime & " " & iCounter
End If

Next

End Sub
```

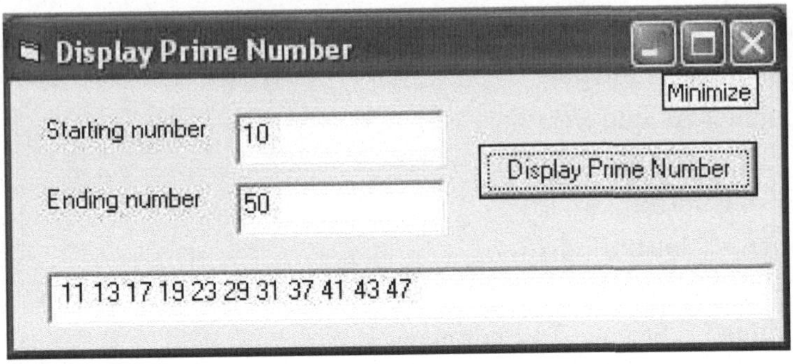

Q9. Write a program in VB to create a login from for IGN OU students like

Passwords of students should be stored properly and on successful login should print message "Successful Login" else "Password or other details are incorrect".

[June 2004, Set-3]

Ans. This Visual Basic application is made for IGNOU student's login process. This application is made on the assumption that the Student details are stored in the database and student login process is validate according to the stored data.

Data Dictionary

Student

Name	Program	Enrollment No.	Password
Saumil	BCA	9810001234	saumil007
Kiran	CIC	9823412392	Km2022

This table contains information regarding the students of IGNOU.
Form frmLogin is design to take student information and validates his/her detail and also provide appropriate message to student.

frmLogin has a command button object to validate the user and four text box objects to take student details.

Object	Description	Name	Properties
Form	Contain application that take student detail and check his/her validation	frmLogin	**Name:** frmLogin **Caption:** Login Form **Height:** 3030 **Width:** 3600
Text	Get the student name	txtName	**Name:** txtName **Text:**
Text	Get the student's program name	txtProgramme	**Name:** txtProgramme **Text:**
Text	Get the student enrollment number	txtNo	**Name:** txtNo **Text:**
Text	Get the student's password	txtPassword	**Name:** txtPassword **Text:** **PasswordChar:** *
Command	To do validate user	cmdLogin	**Name:** cmdLogin **Caption:** Login

Source Code

```
Dim con As New ADODB.Connection
Dim rs As New ADODB.Recordset
Dim sql As String

Private Sub cmdLogin_Click( )

con.open      "Provider=Microsoft.Jet.OLEDB.4.0;   Data Source ="
```

```
& App.Path & "/IGNOU.mdb;Persist Security Info=False"
sql = "select Password from student where Program=" & txtProgramme
& " " and EnrollmentNum = "' & txtNo & " "
rs.Open sql, con, adOpenDynamic, adLockOptimistic

If Not rs.EOF Then
If rs.Fields(0).Value = txtPassword Then
MsgBox "Valid User", vbInformation, "User Login"
Else
MsgBox "Wrong Enrollment Number or Password", vbInformation, "User
Login"
End If
End If

End Sub
```

Q10. Write a program to calculate the Simple Interest on the loan amount using the formula:

I = P * R (Days/365)

Where I = Interest

P = Principal Amount

R = Annual Rate

Days = No. of Days

User will provide all the details like Principal Amount, Annual Rate and Days.

Calculate and display the Simple Interest using text box for inputs and labels for outputs.

[June 2004, Set-4]

Ans. Form frmInterestCalculation is design to take Principal Amount, Annual Rate, Days from the user and calculate the simple interest.

frmInterestCalculation has a command button object to calculate the simple interest and four text box objects to take Principal Amount, Annual Rate, Days from the user.

Object	Description	Name	Properties
Form	Contain application that take Principal Amount, Annual Rate, Days from the user and calculate the simple interest	frmInterestCalculation	**Name:** frmInterestCalculation **Caption:** Interest Calculation **Height:** 2790 **Width:** 3375
Text	Get the principal amount from the user	txtPrincipalAmount	**Name:** txtPrincipalAmount **Text:**
Text	Get the annual rate from the user	txtAnnualRate	**Name:** txtAnnualRate **Text:**
Text	Get the days from the user	txtDays	**Name:** txtDays **Text:**
Text	To display the simple interest	txtInterest	**Name:** txtInterest **Text:**
Command	To calculate the simple interest	cmdCalculateInterest	**Name:** cmdCalculateInterest **Caption:** Calculate Interest

Source Code

```
Private Sub cmdCalculateInterest_Click( )

txtinterest = Round(Val(txtPrincipalAmount) * (Val(txtAnnualRate) / 100)
* (Val(txtDays) / 365), 2)

End Sub
```

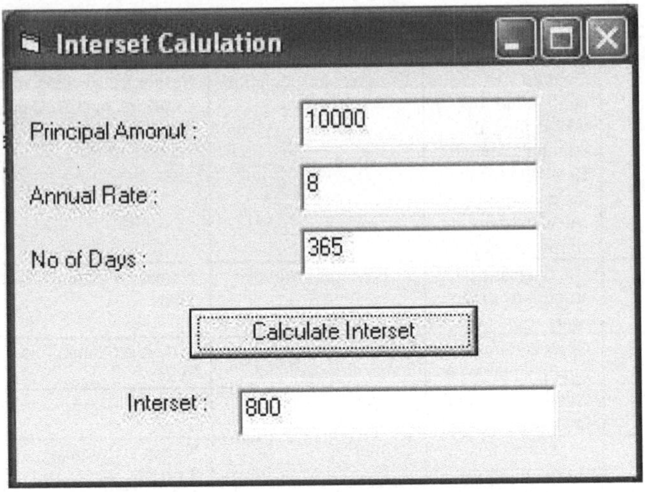

Q11. Write a program in VB which converts the Repeated Integers to the balanced and short form of large integer value. (max value can be 26 integer places) For example

User input: 22266666444444433222225

Output: C2E6G4B3E25

Write one more function in the same program, which converts the "short form" into the actual form.

[June 2004, Set-4]

Ans. Form frmShortForm is design to take input from the user and display short form of large integer value.

frmShortForm has a command button object to display short form of large integer value and two text box objects to take input from the user and second for display the short form of large integer value.

Object	Description	Name	Properties
Form	Contain application that converts the Repeated Integers to the balanced and short form of large integer value	frmShortForm	**Name:** frmShortForm **Caption:** Interest Calculation **Height:** 2790 **Width:** 3375
Text	Get the input from the user	txtInput	**Name:** txtInput **Text:**
Text	To display the short form of large interest value to the user	txtOutput	**Name:** txtOutput **Text:**
Command	To converts the Repeated Integers to the balanced and short form of large integer value	cmdDisplay	**Name:** cmdDisplay **Caption:** Display Short Form

Source Code

```
Function GetShortForm(number As String) As String
Dim c As String
Dim p As String
Dim i As Integer
Dim cnt As Integer
Dim shFrm As String
p = Mid(number, 1, 1)
cnt = 1
For i = 2 To Len(number)
c = Mid(number, i, 1)
If p = c Then
cnt = cnt + 1
Else
If cnt > 1 Then
```

```
shFrm = shFrm & Chr(cnt + 64) & p
Else
shFrm = shFrm & p
End If
cnt = 1
End If
p = c
Next i
If cnt > 1 Then
shFrm = shFrm & Chr(cnt + 64) & p
Else
shFrm = shFrm & p
End If
GetShortForm = shFrm
End Function

Private Sub cmdDisplay_Click()
txtOutput.Text = GetShortForm(txtInput.Text)
End Sub
```

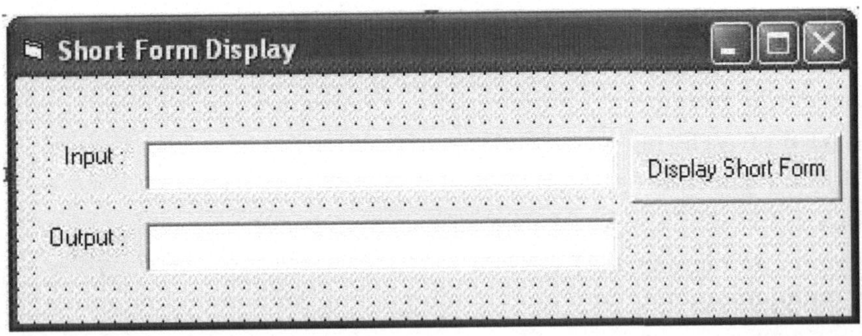

Q12. Create a VB program to calculate a student's grade based on upto 5 projects and 4 tests. Create one or more control arrays of text boxes and appropriate labels to accept the scores gained by the student.

[June 2003, Set-1]

Ans. The Question asks to get the Marks for the 4 tests and 5 Projects. It also asks to calculate the Grade based on the given marks.

• It is also mentioned to used control array for the Text control. Two control arrays are taken:

1. txt_test for get the test marks.

2. txt_prj to get the project marks.

• Grade is calculated from the following formulas

If Per >= 70, then grade = "Distinction"

If Per >= 60, then grade = "First"

If Per >=70. then grade = "Second"

If Per >= 70, then grade = "Pass"

If any marks is below 35, then grade = "Distinction"

The components used to resolve above problem are and its properties are as follow:

• 4 labels show the label "Test 1", "Test 2", "Test 3", "Test4" respectively.

• 5 other labels used to show the label "Project 1", "Project 2", "Project 3", "Project4", "Project 5" respectively.

• Other labels as shown in screen layout

• Other control with its properties are as follow:

Object	Description	Name	Properties
Text	To Input mark for Test1	txt_test(0)	Name: txt_test Text: Index: 0
Text	To Input mark for Test2	txt_test(1)	Name: txt_test Text: Index: 1
Text	To Input mark for Test3.	txt_test(2)	Name: txt_test Text: Index: 2
Text	To Input mark for Test4	txt_test(3)	Name: txt_test Text: Index: 3
Text	To store the total test marks	txt_test(4)	Name: txt_text Text: Index: 4
Text	To Input mark for Project1	txt_prj(0)	Name: txt_prj Text: Index: 0
Text	To Input mark for Project2	txt_prj(1)	Name: txt_prj Text: Index: 1
Text	To Input mark for Project3	txt_prj(2)	Name: txt_prj Text: Index: 2
Text	To Input mark for Project4	txt_prj(3)	Name: txt_prj Text: Index: 3
Text	To Input mark for Project5	txt_prj(4)	Name: txt_prj Text: Index: 4
Text	To store the total of project marks.	txt_prj(5)	Name: txt_prj Text: Index: 5
Text	Total marks (total of test marks + total of Project marks)	txt_total	Name: txt_prj Text: Locked: True
Text	Store the percentage = txt_total/9	txt_per	Name: txt_per Text: Locked: True
Text	Show the calculated Grade based on the input marks	txt_grade	Name: txt_grade Text: Locked: True
Command Button	Provide an Event, at which calculation can be done.	cmd_cal	Name: cmd_cal Caption: &Calculate

Code

```
Private Sub cmd_cal_Click( )
Dim sum As Integer
Dim per As Single
Dim fail As Boolean
fail = False

For i = 0 To 3
sum = sum + Val(txt_test(i).Text)
If Val(txt_test(i).Text) < 35 Then fail = True
Next
txt_test(4) = sum

sum = 0
For i = 0 To 4
sum = sum + Val(txt_prj(i).Text)
If Val(txt_prj(i).Text) < 35 Then fail = True
Next
txt_prj(5) = sum

sum = Val(txt_test(4)) + Val(txt_prj(5))
per = (sum) / 900 * 100

txt_total = sum
txt_per = per

If fail = True Then
txt_grade = "Fail"
Else
Select Case (per)
```

```
Case Is >= 70:
txt_grade = "Distinction"
Case Is >= 60:
txt_grade = "First"
Case Is >= 50:
txt_grade = "Second"
Case Else:
txt_grade = "Pass"
End Select
End If

End Sub
```

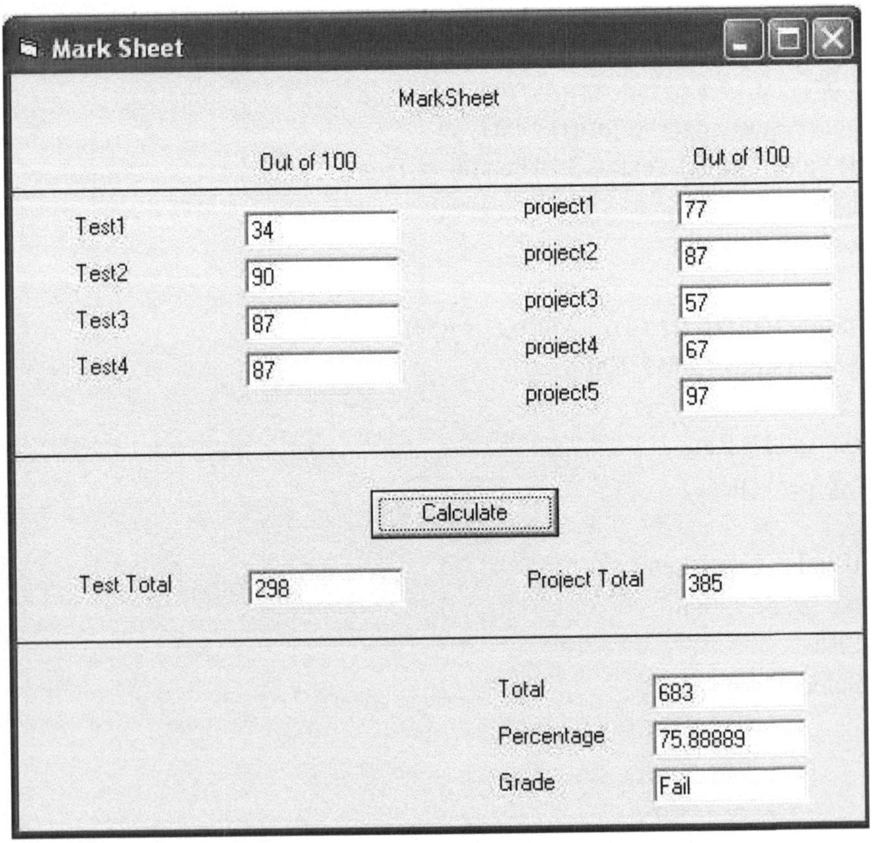

Q13. Write a VB program to collect a positive integer from the user and list all the factors in a multi-line textbox.

Note: the factor of an integer "n" is any integer that divides "n" completely.

Ex: 1, 2, 3 and 6 are the factors of 6.

1, 2, 4, 8 and 16 are the factors of 16.

[June 2003, Set-2]

Ans. The Question asks to get an Input number from the user and find the Factors for that number.

The components used to resolve above problem are and its properties are as follow:

Object	Description	Name	Properties
Text	To Input a number from user.	txt_no	Name: txt_no Text:
Text	To show the factors of a number given in txt_no	txt_factor	Name: txt_factor Text: Locked: True Multiline: True
Command Button	To generate the factors	Command1	Name: Command1 Text: &Generate Factors
Label	Show "Input"	Label1	Name: Label1 Caption: "Input"
Label	Show "Factors"	Label2	Name: Label2 Text: "Factors"

Code

```
Private Sub Command1_Click()
Dim no, i As Integer
no = Val(txt_no.Text)
txt_factor = " "
i = 1

"' check 1 to no number by variable i, if no is divisible by i, add i to txt_factor.
While i <= no

If no Mod i = 0 Then
```

```
txt_factor = txt_factor & i

If i = no Then
txt_factor = txt_factor & "."
Else
txt_factor = txt_factor & ","
End If

End If

i = i + 1
Wend
End Sub
```

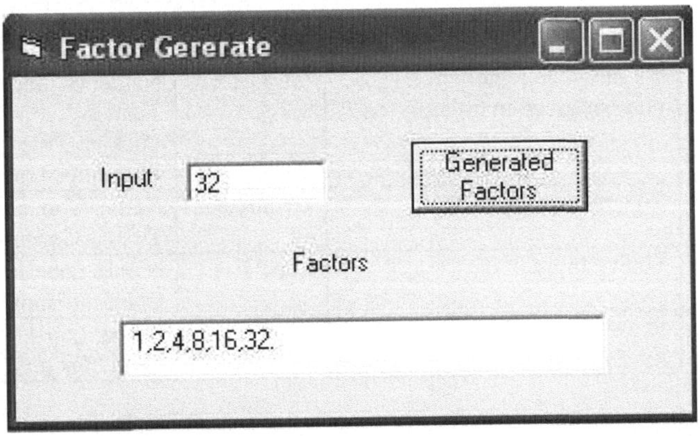

Q14. Create a menu using menu editor.

[June 2003, Set-3]

Ans. To create a menu, one has to follow the following steps:

Step 1: Select a form on which, menu has to be created

Step 2: Open Tool Menu

Step 3: Select a menu option – Menu Editor

Which will display following dialog box to set different Menus.

Step 4: To create each menu, one has to set the fields for the Caption, Name, appropriate Navigation arrow. Next Command button is used for each new Menu or SubMenu.

For Example, to create a Menu as given in Question, one will follow Steps 1, 2 and 3. He has to do following steps to create the entire Menu. The Menu setting for each Menu.

Caption	Name	Shortcut	Indentation for the Hierarchy of Menu	Command Button for the next event
&File	mn_File			Next
&New	mns_File_New	CTRL + N	→	Next
&Open	mns_File_Open	CTRL + O		Next
&Save	mns_File_Save			Next
S&ave as	mns_File_SaAs			Next
E&xit	mns_File_Exit			Next
Edit	mns_Edit		←	Next
&Add	mns_Edit_Add		→	Next
&Change	mns_Edit_Ch			Next
&Delete	mns_Edit_Del			Next
Help	mn_Help		→	Next

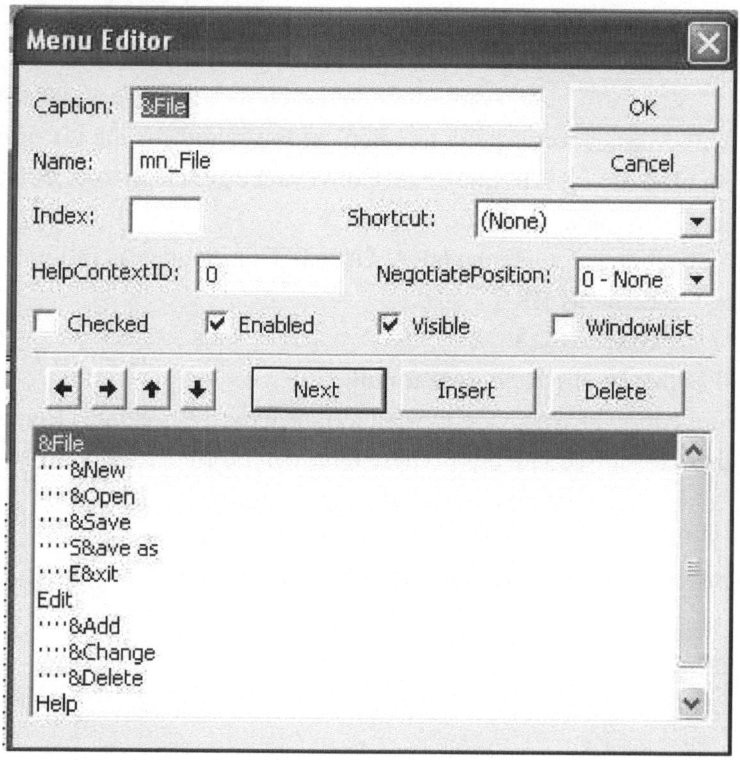

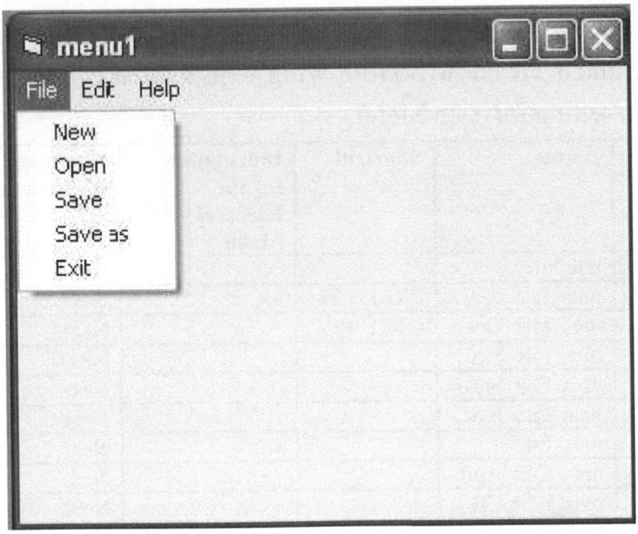

Q15. Develop a small application to find the Gross salary and Net salary by taking the inputs BASIC, HRA, DA, CONVEYANCE and DEDUCTIONS (LIC, INCOME_TAX, LOANS, ETC.)

[Dec 2002, Set-4]

Ans. This Application is used to calculate the salary for the given basic. The Sample Rate for HRA, DA and Conveyance are taken to calculate the basic and net salary.

This application calculate the HRA, DA and Conveyance as follow:

15% of the Basic as HRA

40% of the Basic as DA

Rs.800 as the fixed conveyance for all

This application also provide the deductions like LIC, Income_Tax, Loans and others for miscellaneous). These data will be entered by the user.

Gross and Net Salary are calculated from the following formulas.

Gross Salary = Basic Salary + HRA + DA + Conveyance

Net Salary = Gross Salary – (Loan + Income_tax + LIC + others)

Object	Field	Name	Properties
TextBox	Accept the data for Basic Salary from User	Text_BASIC	Name: Text_BASIC Text: " "
TextBox	Display 15% of the Basic as HRA	Text_HRA	Name: Text_HRA Text: " "
TextBox	Display 40% of the Basic as DA	Text_DA	Name: Text_DA Text: " "
TextBox	Display 800 as Conveyance	Text_Conveyance	Name: Text_Conveyance Text: " "
TextBox	Accept the data for LIC premium paid from the salary	Text_LIC	Name: Text_LIC Text: " "
TextBox	Accept the data for Loan Installments paid from the salary	Text_LOAN	Name: Text_LOAN Text: " "
TextBox	Accept the data for Income Tax paid from the salary	Text_IT	Name: Text_IT Text: " "
TextBox	Accept the data for other deductable expense like (PF, PPF, NSC, Infra. Bond etc.)	Text_Other	Name: Text_Other Text: " "
TextBox	Show calculated Gross salary	Text_GRSAL	Name: Text_GRSAL Text: " "
TextBox	Show calculated Net salary	Text_NETSAL	Name: Text_NETSAL Text: " "
Command	Command button used to provide an event to calculate the data	CALCULATE	Name: Calculate Caption: &Calculate

Source code

```
Private Sub CALCULATE_Click( )
'" Prompt for Basic Data (that is compulsory)

If Text_BASIC = " " Then
MsgBox "Basic Must be specified"
Text_BASIC.SetFocus
Exit Sub
End If
```

```
If Text_LIC = " " Then
Text_LIC = 0
End If

If Text_IT = " " Then
Text_IT = 0
End If

If Text_OTHERS = " " Then
Text_OTHERS = 0
End If

If text_LOANS = " " Then
Text_LOANS = 0
End If

Text_HRA = Text_BASIC * 15/100
Text_DA = Text_BASIC * 40/100
Text_CONVEYANCE = Text_BASIC * 10/100
Text_GRSAL = CSng(Text_BASIC) + CSng(Text_HRA) +
CSng(Text_DA) + CSng(Text_CONVEYANCE)
Text_NETSAL = CSng(Text_GRSAL) – CSng(Text_LIC) –
CSng(Text_IT) – CSng(Text_LOANS) – CSng(Text_OTHERS)
End Sub
```

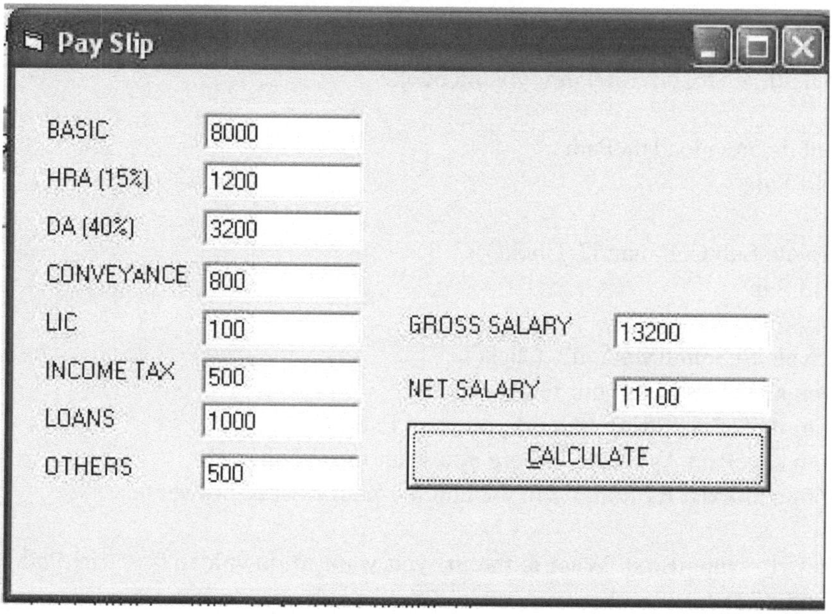

Q16. Shows two ways to download a url/file from the internet via api.

Ans. Private Declare Function DoFileDownload Lib "shdocvw.dll" (ByVal lpszFile As String) As Long
Private Declare Function URLDownloadToFile Lib "urlmon" Alias "URLDownloadToFileA" (ByVal pCaller As Long, ByVal szURL As String, ByVal szFileName As String, ByVal dwReserved As Long, ByVal lpfnCB As Long) As Long

Private Sub Command1_Click()
End Sub

Private Sub cmdMethod1_Click()
Dim thePath As String
thePath = InputBox("What is the url to download the file?", " File Url", "http:/

```
/")

'The path has to be converted to Unicode
thePath = StrConv(thePath, vbUnicode)

DoFileDownload thePath
End Sub

Private Sub Command2_Click()
End Sub

Private Sub cmdMethod2_Click()
Dim retVal As Long 'our return value
Dim theUrl As String 'the url you want to download
Dim savePath As String 'where you want to save the url
Dim pathExist As Long 'will contain our path exist or not value

theUrl = InputBox("What is the url you want to download?", " Url Path?",
"http://")
If theUrl = "" Then Exit Sub

savePath = InputBox("What is the path and filename to save the url to?", "
Path and Filename to save")
If savePath = "" Then Exit Sub

retVal = URLDownloadToFile(0, theUrl, savePath, 0, 0)

If retVal = 0 Then
MsgBox "File was downloaded successfully!", vbExclamation, " Download
Successful"
Else
MsgBox "There was a error downloading the file. Make sure that the url is
valid and try again!", vbCritical, " Error"
End If
End Sub
'
```

Q17. This program checks if User is Active.

Ans.

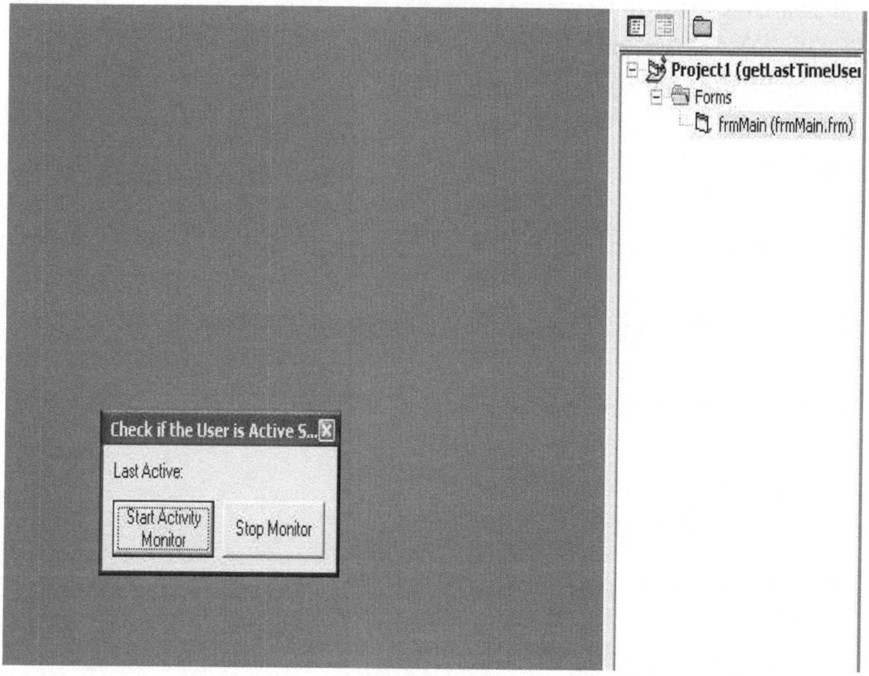

A small example that shows how to determine whether the user is active or inactive
'in Windows. IF the user is not active, then it will provide the tick count time they were last
'active.
'
'Structure passed to the GetLastInput API Function.
Private Type inputInfo

structSize As Long

tickCount As Long

End Type

```
'
'The variable that will be passed to the API call and receive the activity report.
Private info As inputInfo
Private Declare Function GetLastInputInfo Lib "user32.dll" (inputStructure As inputInfo) As _
   Boolean
'
Dim firstTick As Long
'
Dim lastTick As Long
'
Private Sub cmdStart_Click()
'
'Begin the Activity Monitor.
tmr.Enabled = True

End Sub

Private Sub cmdStop_Click()
'
'Stop the timer monitor.
tmr.Enabled = False

End Sub

Private Sub Form_Load()
End Sub

Private Sub lblTime_Click()

End Sub

'
'Will hold the tickcount value returned from the API call.
```

```
'
Private Sub tmr_Timer()
'
'This timer will fire every 1000ms(One Second) or so displaying the last time the user was
'active.
'
'The size of the structure for the API call.
info.structSize = Len(info)
'
'Call the API.
GetLastInputInfo info
'
'Compare the tickcount values to determine if activity has occurred or not.
If firstTick <> info.tickCount Then
'
'Display the current time of the users last activity.
lblTime.Caption = "Last Active: " & Time
'
'Get the new tick value.
firstTick = info.tickCount

End If

End Sub
```

Q18. Example of Generating Tones.

Ans.

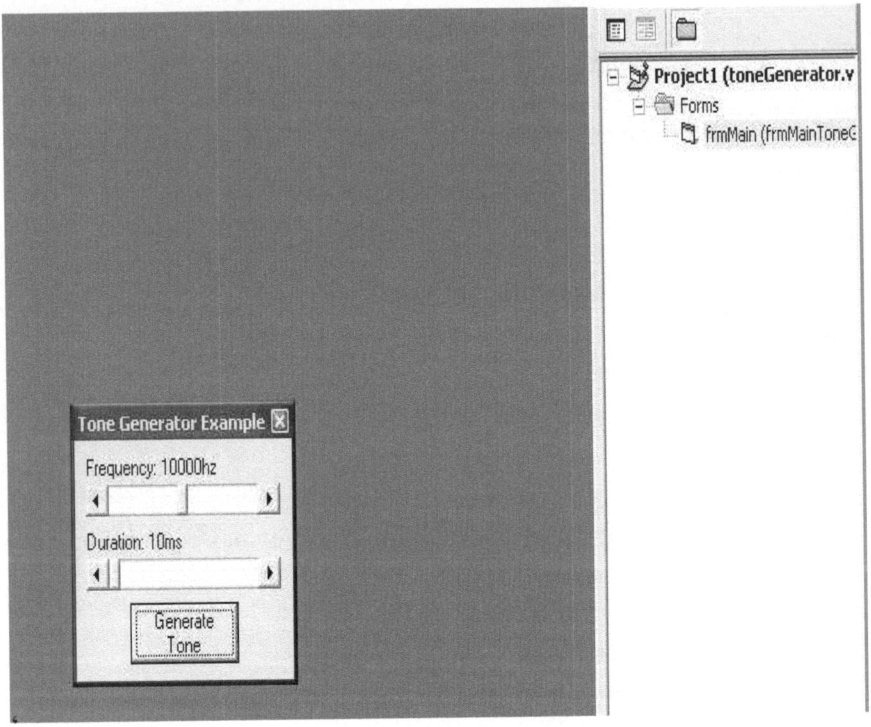


```
'Description: Example on how to create simple tones using
'the Beep Api Function. There are lots of hardware out
'there that may support different frequencys. So, you will
'have to see how high/low the frequencys are that your
'hardware supports then change the min/max frequency
'values to your hardware.
'
'This example could be used for morse code or something.
'Have fun.

Private Declare Function Beep Lib "kernel32" (ByVal dwFreq As Long, ByVal
dwDuration As Long) As Long

Private Sub cmdGenerate_Click()
   Beep hsFreq.Value, hsDur.Value
End Sub
Private Sub Form_Load()
```

```
End Sub

Private Sub hsDur_Change()
  lblDuration = "Duration: " & hsDur.Value & "ms"
End Sub

Private Sub hsFreq_Change()
  lblFreq.Caption = "Frequency: " & hsFreq.Value & "hz"
End Sub
```

Now Refer solution of Q2 in this chapter.

Question Papers

CS-65 : Windows Programming
December, 2006

Note : There are 2 questions in this paper. Answer both the questions. They carry 50 marks. The rest 25 marks are for the viva-voce.

SET - 1

Q1. Simulate a simple polling application and draw the result basing upon the votes gained by the individual Candidates. Assumptions can be made wherever necessary. **25**

Ans. Design Window

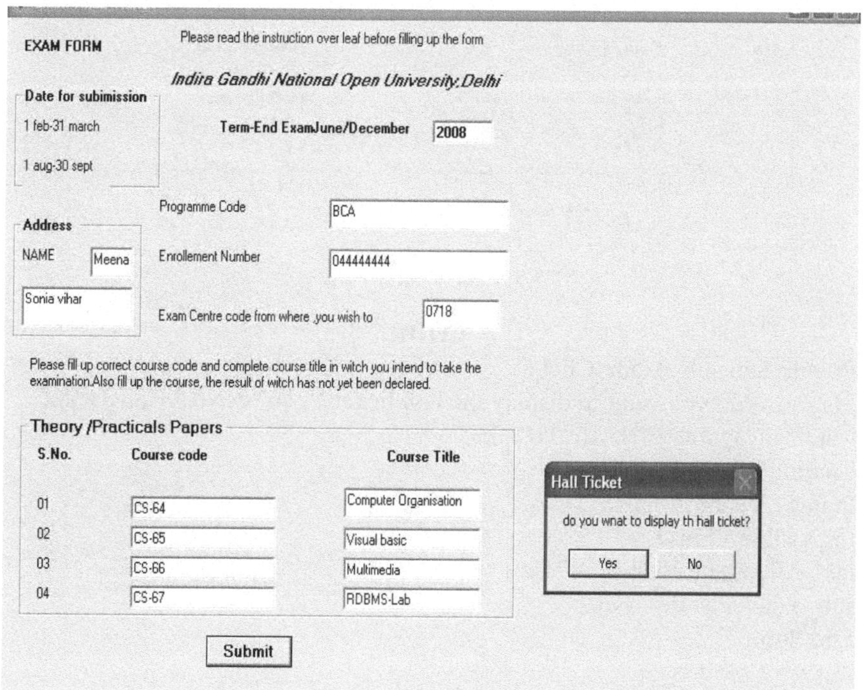

HALL-TICKET

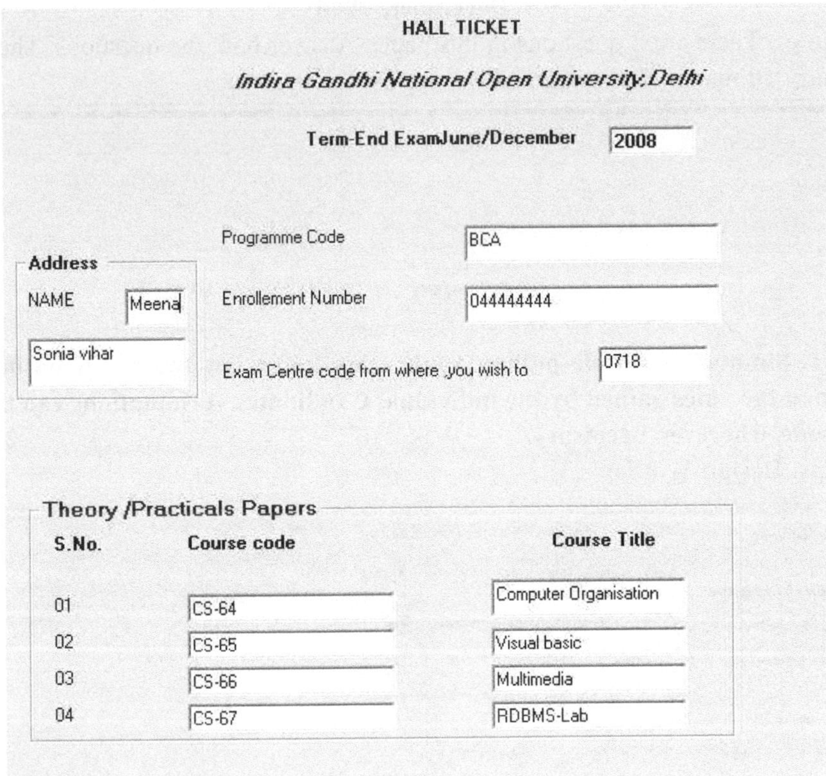

CODE

```
Private Sub sub_exam_Click()
MsgBox "do you want to display the hall ticket?", vbYesNo, "Hall Ticket"
heading.Caption = "HALL TICKET"
heading.FontBold = True
Frame2.Visible = False
ins.Visible = False
ins1.Alignment.Visible = False
sub_exam.Visible = False
End Sub
```

Q2. Write a program in VB program to count the number of words in a sentence .If the sentence is to be ended with a "." (Period).

Ans. Design Window

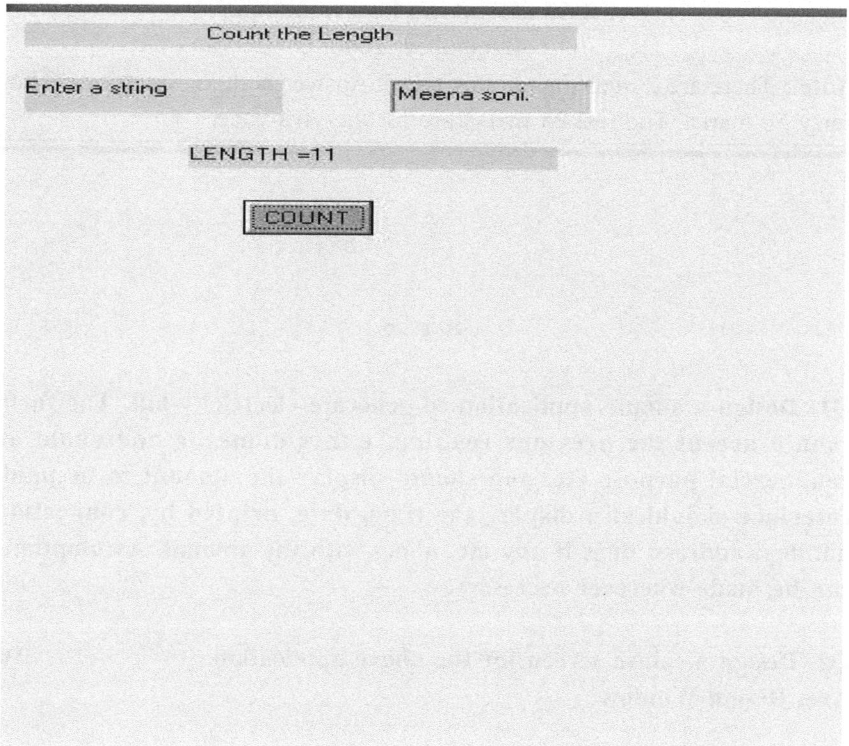
Count the Length
Enter a string
Meena soni.
LENGTH =11
COUNT

CS-65 : Windows Programming
December, 2006

Note : There are 2 questions in this paper. Answer both the questions. They carry 50 marks. The rest 25 marks are for the viva-voce.

SET - 2

Q1. Design a simple application to generate electricity-bill. The form should accept the previous reading; either domestic household or commercial purpose etc. and should display the amount to be paid. Interface should also display the time, date, printed by, connection number, address, dues if any etc. along with the amount. Assumptions can be made wherever necessary. **40**

Q2. Design a splash-screen for the above application. **10**

Ans. Design Window

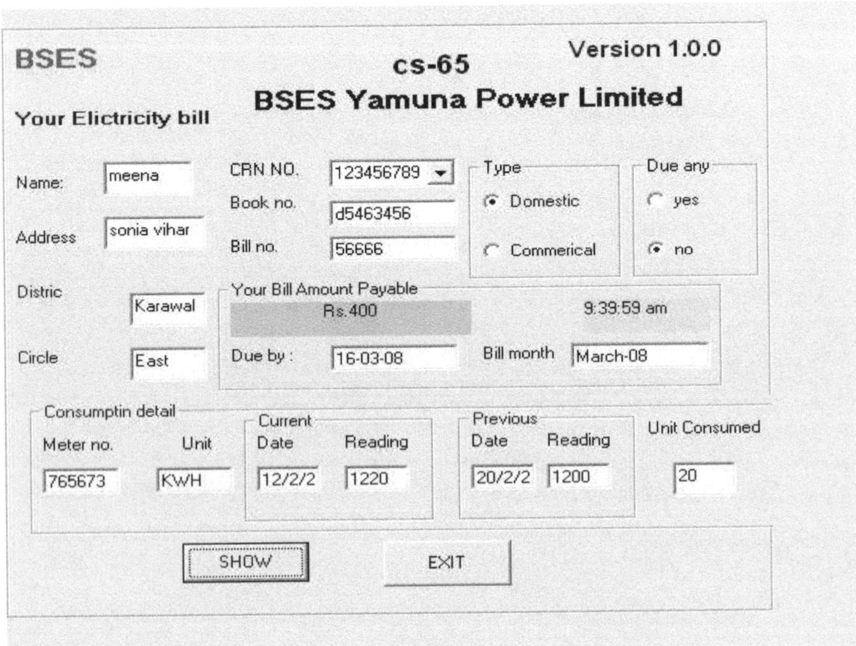

CODE

```
Option Explicit
Private Sub Cr_no_Click ()
If Cr_no.Text = "1234567890" Then
Name. Text "meena"
add. Text = "sonia vihar"
bk_no.Text = "d5463456"
bl_no.Text = "56666"
dis.Text = "Karawal nagar"
cir.Text = "East"
m_no.Text = "765673"
unt.Text = "KWH"
End If
If Cr_no.Text = "9876543212" Then
name.Text = "beena"
add.Text = "Nehru vihar"
bk_no.Text = "dt463456"
bl_no.Text = "554358"
dis.Text = "Karawal nagar"
cir.Text = "East"
m_no.Text = "777673"
unt.Text = "KWH"
End If
If Cr_no.Text = "6737487346" Then
name.Text = "Neena"
add.Text = "Prasant vihar"
bk_no.Text = "tl463456"
bl_no.Text = "564358"
dis.Text = "Karawal nagar"
cir.Text = "west"
m_no.Text = "456346"
unt.Text = "MWH"
End If
End Sub

Private Sub exit_Click()
End
End Sub

Private Sub Form_Load()
```

```
  lblVersion.Caption = "Version " & App.Major & "." & App.Minor & "." &
App.Revision
  lblProductName.Caption = App.Title
   c_date.Text = ("12/2/2008")
   p_date.Text = ("20/2/2008")
    due.Text = Format(Now, "dd-mm-yy")
    b_month.Text = Format(Now, "mmmm-yy")
   time.Caption = Format(Now, "h:mm:ss am/pm")
End Sub

Private Sub dom_Click()
   Cr_no.AddItem ("1234567890")
   Cr_no.AddItem ("9876543212")
   Cr_no.AddItem ("2356218760")
   name.Text = ""
   add.Text = ""
   bk_no.Text = ""
   bl_no.Text = ""
   dis.Text = ""
   cir.Text = ""
   m_no.Text = ""
   unt.Text = ""
End Sub

Private Sub com_Click()
   Cr_no.AddItem ("6737487346")
   Cr_no.AddItem ("5456355769")
   Cr_no.AddItem ("5564645555")
   name.Text = ""
   add.Text = ""
   bk_no.Text = ""
   bl_no.Text = ""
   dis.Text = ""
   cir.Text = ""
   m_no.Text = ""
   unt.Text = ""
End Sub

Private Sub show_Click()
u_c.Text = Val(c_read.Text) - Val(p_read.Text)
amount.Caption = "Rs." & 20 * u_c.Text
End sub
```

CS-65 : Windows Programming
December, 2006

Note : There are 2 questions in this paper. Answer both the questions. They carry 50 marks. The rest 25 marks are for the viva-voce.

SET - 3

Q1. Design a simple application to display the hall-ticket. The basis for this is user enters the details in the form of an examination application form. Assumptions can be made wherever necessary

Ans. Design Window

EXAM-FORM

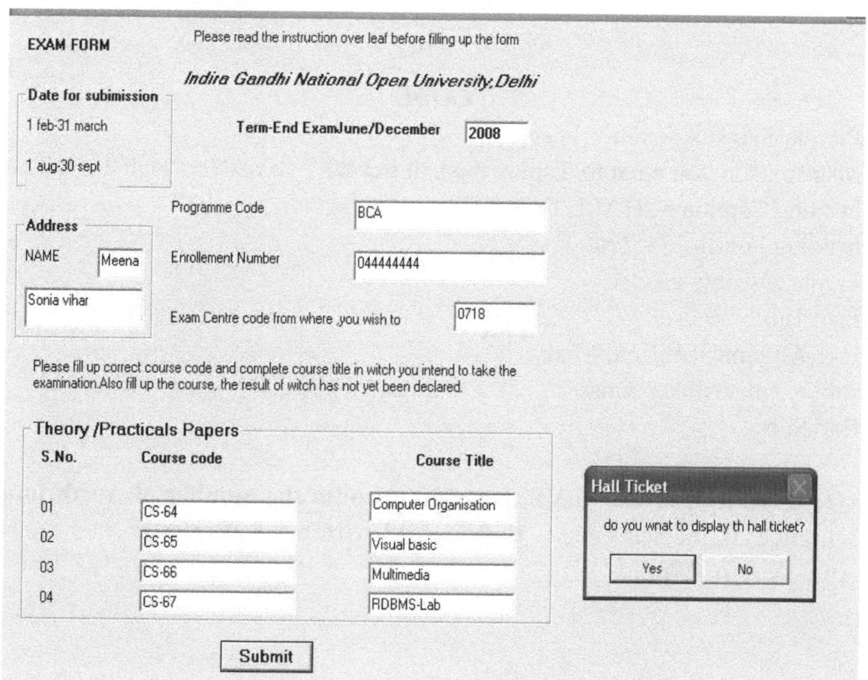

HALL-TICKET

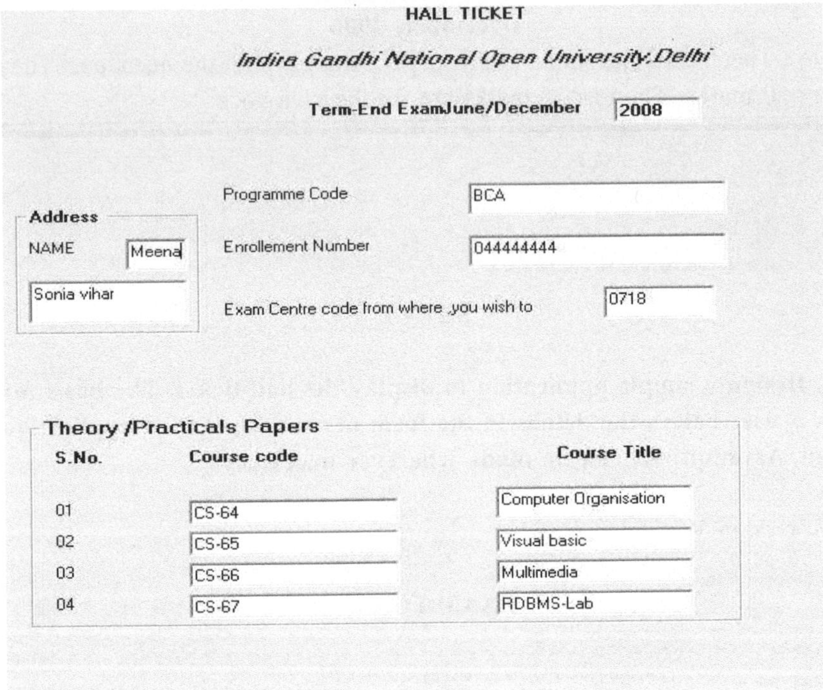

CODE

```
Private Sub sub_exam_Click()
MsgBox "do you wnat to display the hall ticket?", vbYesNo, "Hall Ticket"
heading.Caption = "HALL TICKET"
heading.FontBold = True
Frame2.Visible = False
ins.Visible = False
ins1.Alignment.Visible = False
sub_exam.Visible = False
End Sub
```

Q2. Write a program in VB program to count the number of words in a sentence. If the sentence is to be ended with a "." (Period).

Ans. Design Window

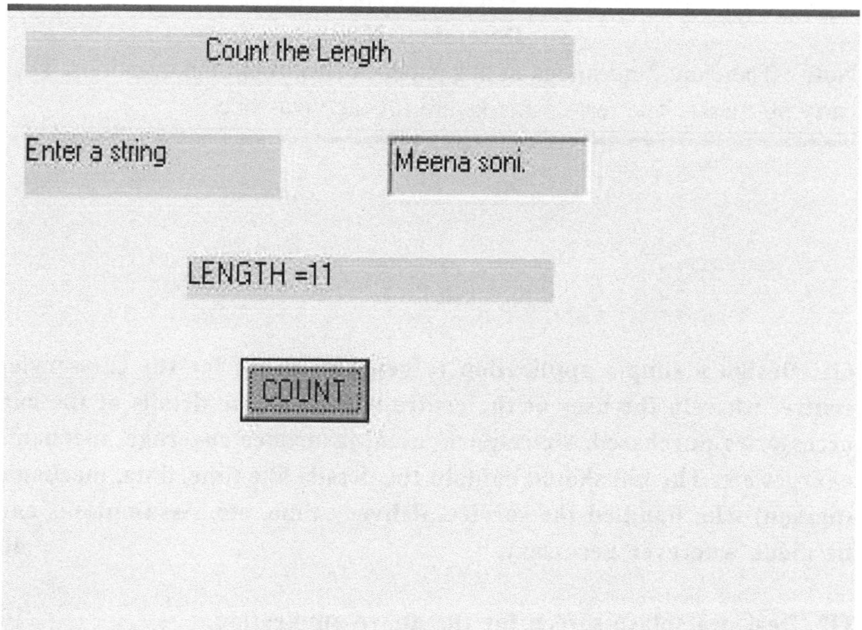

CODE

```
Private Sub Cmd_count_Click ()
Dim a As String
a = Txtlen.Text
Length. Caption = "LENGTH =" & Len (a)
End Sub
```

CS-65 : Windows Programming
December, 2006

Note : There are 2 questions in this paper. Answer both the questions. They carry 50 marks. The rest 25 marks are for the viva-voce.

SET - 4

Q1. Design a simple application to generate a bill for the car-service centre, wherein the user at the centre will input the details of the car, accessories purchased, spare-parts used, insurance coverage, mechanic charges etc. The bill should contain the details like time, date, mechanic (person) who handled the service, delivery time, etc. Assumptions can be made wherever necessary. **40**

Q2. Design a splash-screen for the above application. **10**

Ans. Design Window

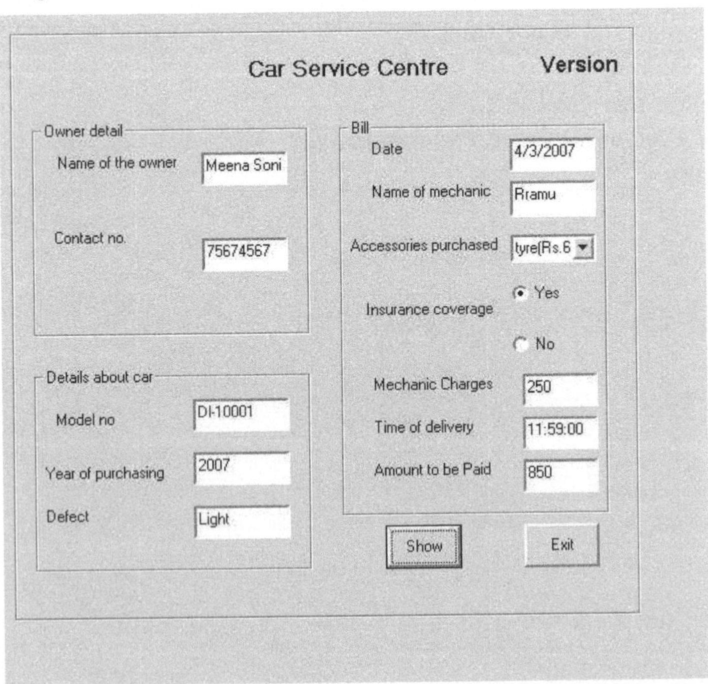

CODE

```
Private Sub Command1_Click()
If Combo1.Text = Combo1.List(0) Then
Text10.Text = Val(Text8.Text) + 35000
ElseIf Combo1.Text = Combo1.List(1) Then
Text10.Text = Val(Text8.Text) + 20000
ElseIf Combo1.Text = Combo1.List(2) Then
Text10.Text = Val(Text8.Text) + 50
Else
Text10.Text = Val(Text8.Text) + 600
End If
End Sub

Private Sub Command2_Click ()
End
End Sub

Private Sub Form Load ()
Combo1.AddItem ("AC (Rs.35000/-)")
Combo1.AddItem ("Music System (Rs.20000/-)")
Combo1.AddItem ("Breaks oil (Rs.50/-)")
Combo1.AddItem ("tyre (Rs.600/-)")
Text6.Text = Date
Text9.Text = Time ()
End Sub
```

CS-65 : Windows Programming
June, 2007

Note : There are 2 questions in this paper. Answer both the questions. They carry 50 marks. The rest 25 marks are for the viva-voce.

SET - 1

Q1. Create a form with a picture-box. Find 3 interesting pictures and use a timer control to cycle these 3 pictures every one second. Place an exit button to close the application. **25**

Ans. Design Window

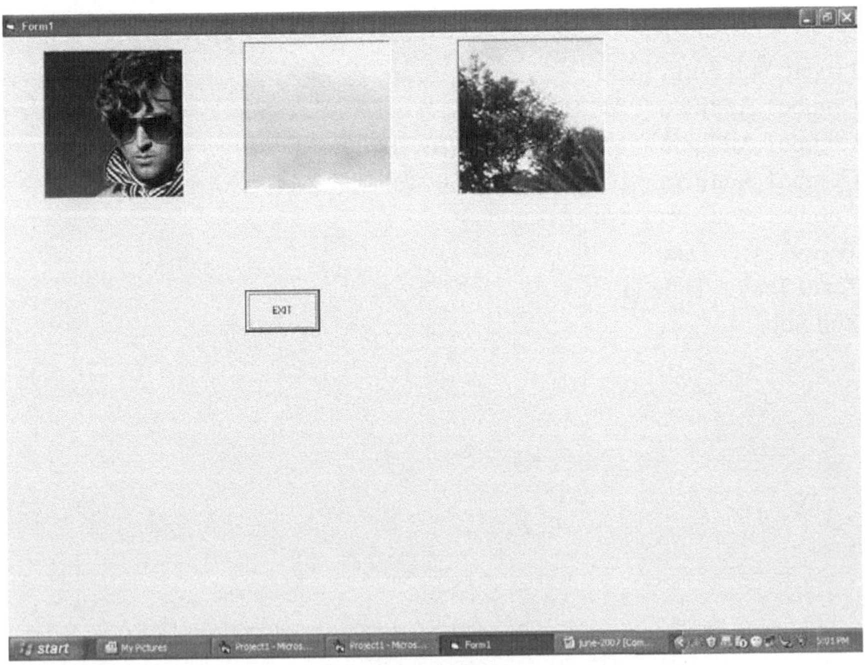

CODE Window

```
Private Sub Timer1_Timer()
```

```
Dim a, b As Byte
a = a + 1

If a = 4 Then
a = 1
End If

If a = 1 Then
Form1.Picture = LoadPicture("C:\Documents and Settings\All
Users\Documents\My Pictures\Sample Pictures")
a = a + 1
End If

If a = 2 Then
Form1.Picture = LoadPicture("C:\Documents and Settings\All
Users\Documents\My Pictures\Sample Pictures")
a = a + 1
End If

If a = 3 Then
Form1.Picture = LoadPicture("C:\Documents and Settings\All Users\
Documents\My Pictures\Sample Pictures")
End If
End Sub
Private Sub Command1_Click()
End
End Sub
```

Q2. Write an event procedure to display the type of the triangle, given the measurements of its 3 sides by the user.
Note: A triangle is said to be an equilateral triangle if all its sides are equal, an isosceles' triangle if any two sides are equal and a scalene triangle if all of its sides are unequal. Design a very interactive user interface. 25

Ans. Design Window

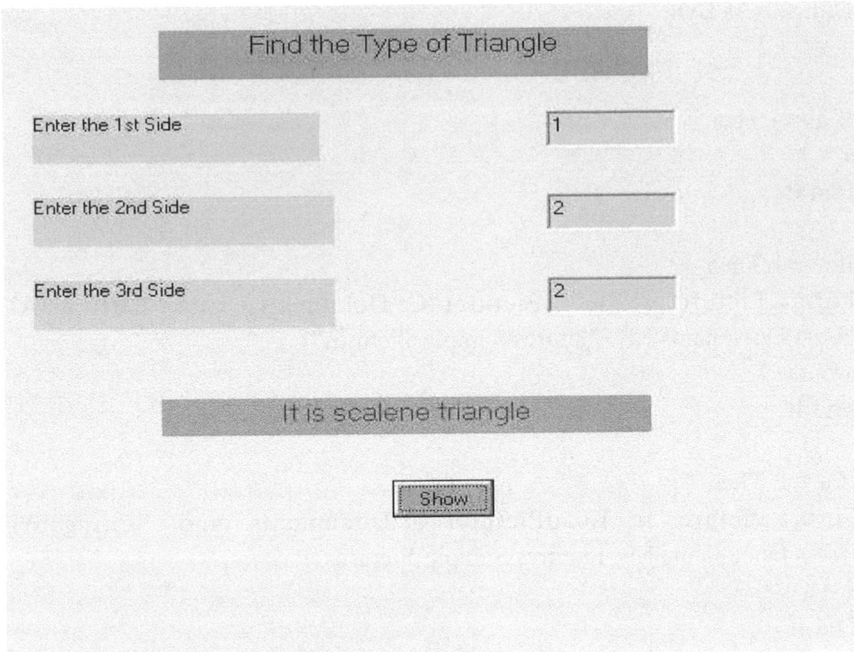

CODE

```
Private Sub Cmd_show_Click()
Dim a, b, c As Integer
a = Val(Text1.Text)
b = Val(Text2.Text)
c = Val(Text3.Text)
If ((a = b) And (a = c)) Then
Label5.Caption = "It is equilateral triangle "
End If
If ((a = b) And (a <> c)) Then
Label5.Caption = "It is isosceles triangle "
End If
If ((a <> b) And (a = c)) Then
Label5.Caption = "It is isosceles triangle "
End If
If ((a <> b) And (a <> c)) Then
Label5.Caption = "It is scalene triangle"
End If
End Sub
```

CS-65 : Windows Programming
June, 2007

Note : There are 2 questions in this paper. Answer both the questions. They carry 50 marks. The rest 25 marks are for the viva-voce.

SET - 2

Q1. Create a form where the user enter some text into a text-box control and have the result output into a label in a different font with the colour change in the background of the form. **25**

Ans. Design Window

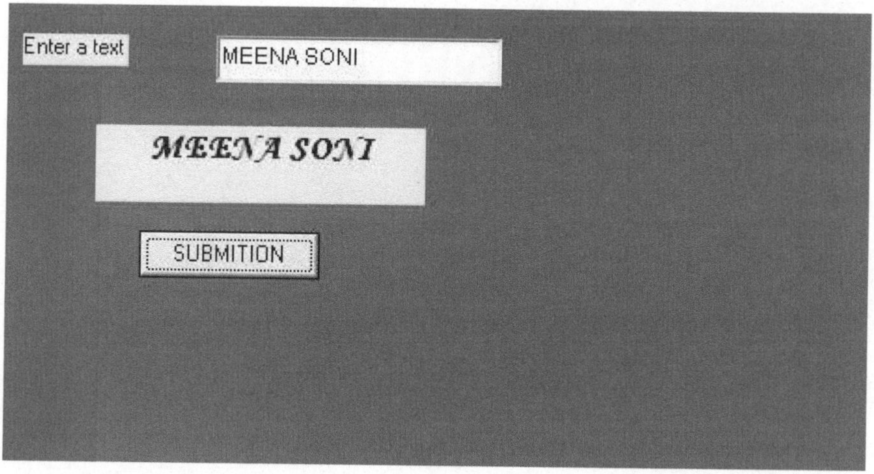

CODE

```
Private Sub Command1_Click ()
Label2.Caption = UCase (Text1.Text)
```

```
Me.BackColor = vbRed
End Sub
```

Q2. Write an event procedure to collect an, integer from the user and find out whether the given integer is an odd integer or an even one. Design a splash screen for this application. Use appropriate controls on the form. 25

Ans. Design Window Splash screen

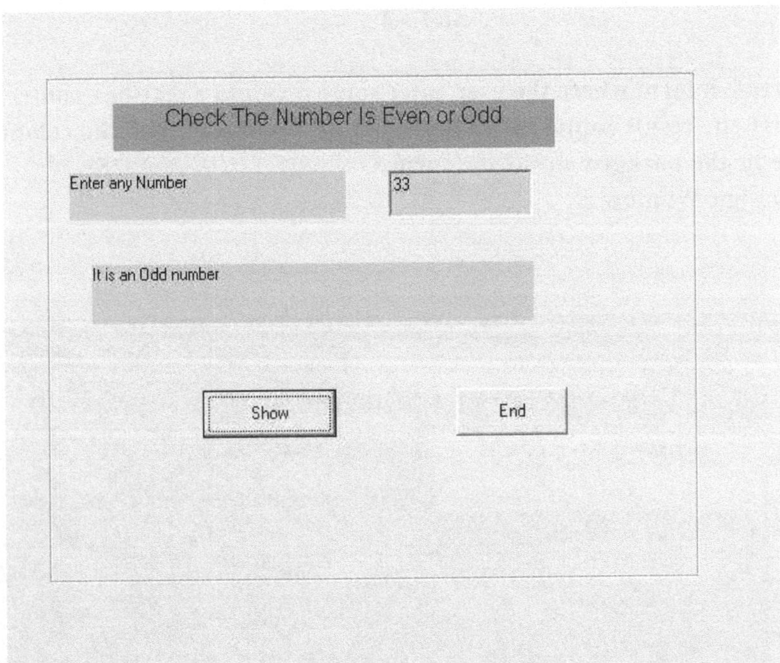

CODE

```
Private Sub Cmd_show_Click()
Dim a As Integer
a = Text1.Text
If a Mod 2 = 0 Then
Label3.Caption = "It is an even number"
```

```
End If
If a Mod 2 <> 0 Then
Label3.Caption = "It is an Odd number"
End If
End Sub

Private Sub Cmd_end_Click()
End
End Sub
```

CS-65 : Windows Programming
June, 2007

Note : There are 2 questions in this paper. Answer both the questions. They carry 50 marks. The rest 25 marks are for the viva-voce.

SET - 3

Q1. Collect the first name, middle name and the last name from the user on 'three separate text-boxes and display the user's short name.

Ans. Design Window

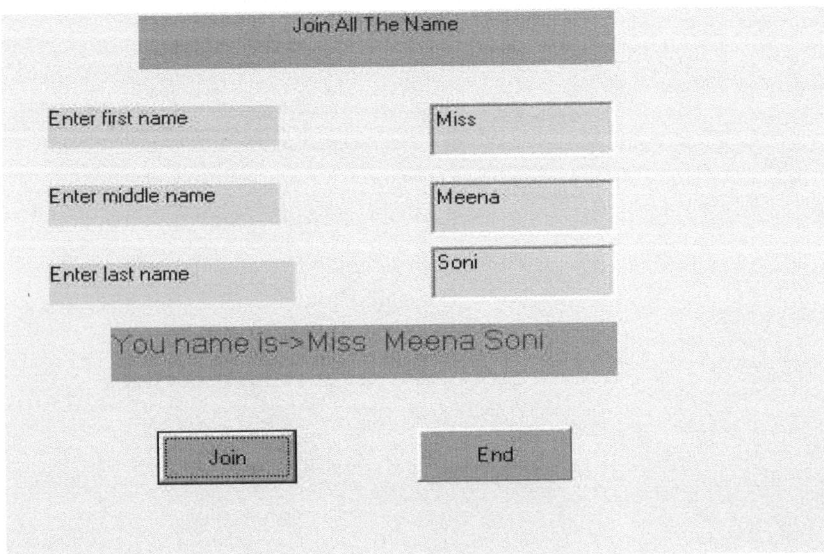

CODE

```
Private Sub cmd_join_Click()
Dim a, b, c As String
a = Text1.Text
b = Text2.Text
```

```
c = Text3.Text
Label2.Caption = "You name is->" & a & " " & b & " " & c
End Sub
Private Sub Cmd_end_Click()
End
End Sub
```

Q2. Write a Visual Basic program to compute the FV (Future Value) of an investment. The formula to be used is as follows:
FV - Investment * (1 + Interest RatelYfare,
Also, design a splash screen for this application. Use appropriate controls to design the User Interface
Ans. Design Window

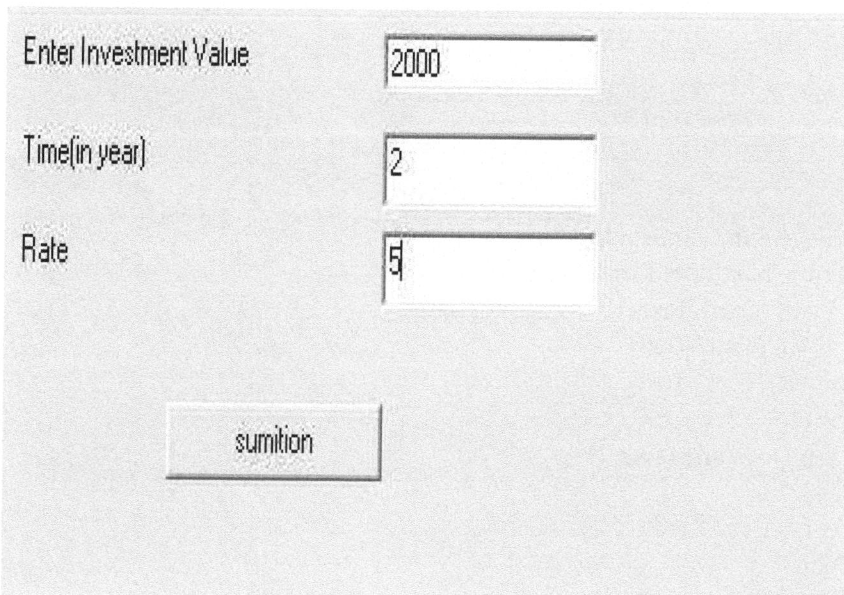

Splash screen

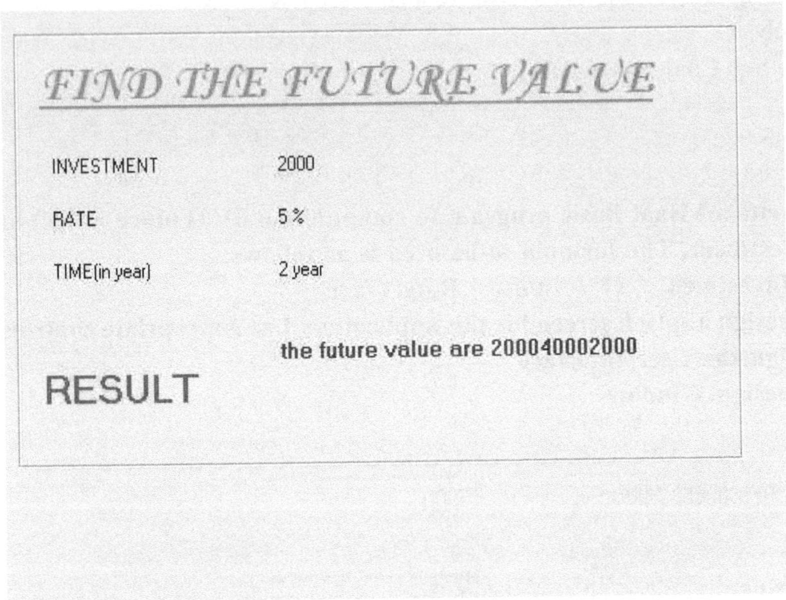

CODE

```
Private Sub Command1_Click ()
Dim a, b, c, d, e, f as Integer
a = Val (Text1.Text)
b = Val (Text2.Text)
c = Val (Text3.Text)
e = (1 + a * c)
f = b Do While (f <> 1)
e = e * e
f = f – 1
Loop
d = a * e
frmS.Label7.Caption = STR (a)
frmS.Label8.Caption = STR(c) + "%"
frmS.Label9.Caption = STR (b) + "year"
frmS.Label1.Caption = "the future value are" + STR (Format (d,
"#########.00"))
frmS.Show
End Sub
```

CS-65 : Windows Programming
June, 2007

Note : There are 2 questions in this paper. Answer both the questions. They carry 50 marks. The rest 25 marks are for the viva-voce.

SET - 4

Q1. Design a simple application to generate a bill for a stationery shop which sells books, CD's, DVD's, writing pads, pens pencils and other stationery items. Assumptions can be made, wherever necessary. 25

Ans. Design Window

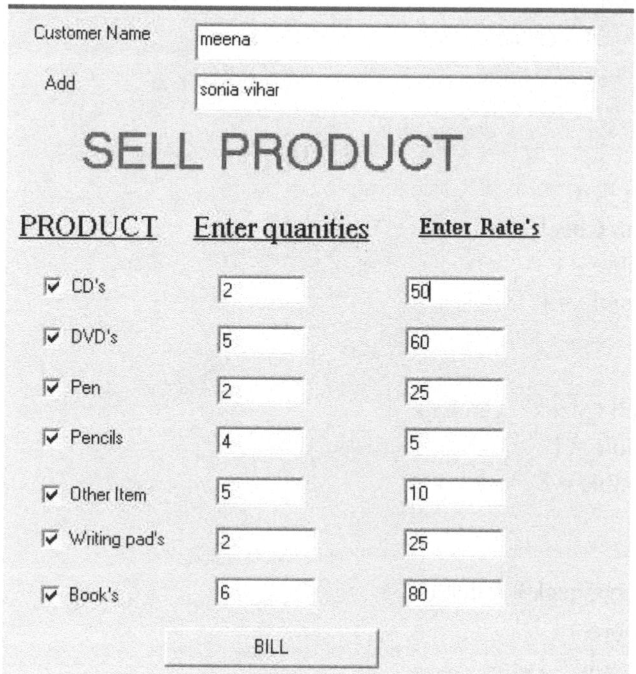

SPLASH SCREEN

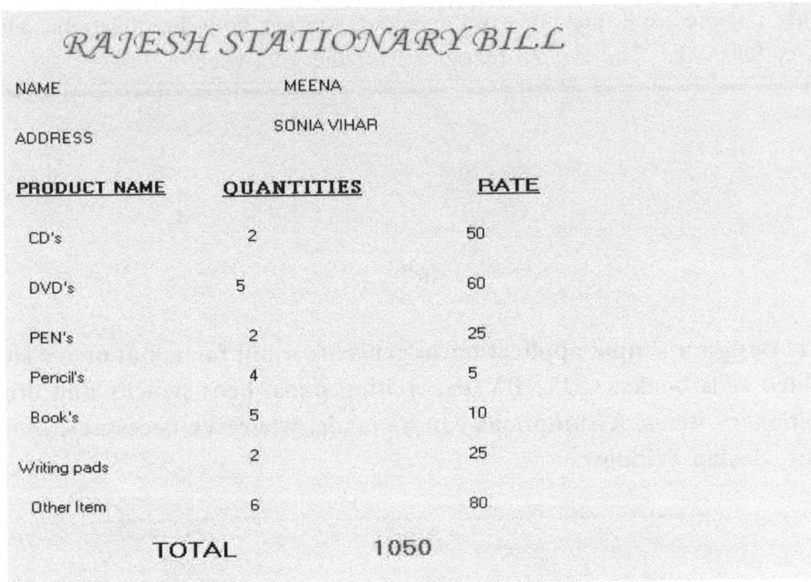

CODE

```
Option Explicit
Private Sub Check1_Click ()
Text3.Visible = 1
Text10.Visible = 1
End Sub

Private Sub Check2_Click ()
Text4.Visible = 1
Text11.Visible = 1
End Sub

Private Sub Check3_Click ()
Text5.Visible = 1
Text12.Visible = 1

End Sub
```

```
Private Sub Check4_Click ()
Text6.Visible = 1
Text13.Visible = 1

End Sub

Private Sub Check5_Click ()
Text7.Visible = 1
Text14.Visible = 1

End Sub

Private Sub Check6_Click ()
Text8.Visible = 1
Text15.Visible = 1

End Sub

Private Sub Check7_Click ()
Text9.Visible = 1
Text16.Visible = 1

End Sub

Private Sub Command1_Click ()
Dim a, b, c, d, e, f, g, h as Integer
Form2.Label3.Caption = UCase (Text1.Text)
Form2.Label5.Caption = UCase (Text2.Text)
Form2.Label16.Caption = Text3.Text
Form2.Label17.Caption = Text4.Text
Form2.Label18.Caption = Text5.Text
Form2.Label19.Caption = Text6.Text
Form2.Label20.Caption = Text7.Text
Form2.Label21.Caption = Text8.Text
Form2.Label22.Caption = Text9.Text
Form2.Label23.Caption = Text10.Text
Form2.Label24.Caption = Text11.Text
Form2.Label25.Caption = Text12.Text
```

```
Form2.Label26.Caption = Text13.Text
Form2.Label27.Caption = Text14.Text
Form2.Label28.Caption = Text15.Text
Form2.Label29.Caption = Text16.Text
a = Val (Text3.Text) * Val (Text10.Text)
b = Val (Text4.Text) * Val (Text11.Text)
c = Val (Text5.Text) * Val (Text12.Text)
d = Val (Text6.Text) * Val (Text13.Text)
e = Val (Text7.Text) * Val (Text14.Text)
f = Val (Text8.Text) * Val (Text15.Text)
g = Val (Text9.Text) * Val (Text16.Text)
Form2.Label31.Caption = a + b + c + d + e + f + g
Form2.Show
End Sub
```

Q2. Create a VB program to introduce yourself to the lab faculty. When the program is run, it should provide the complete information about you. Design a good interface with appropriate controls on the form. 25

Ans. Design Window

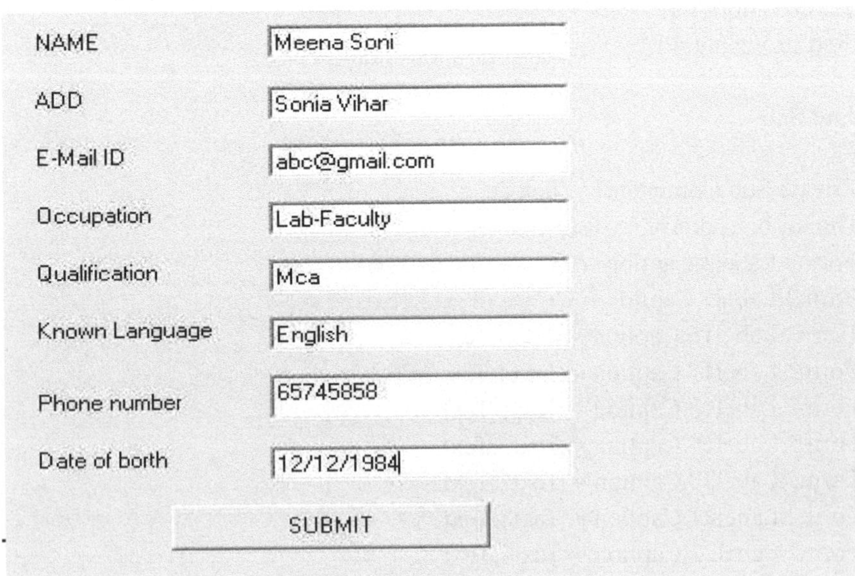

Splash Screen

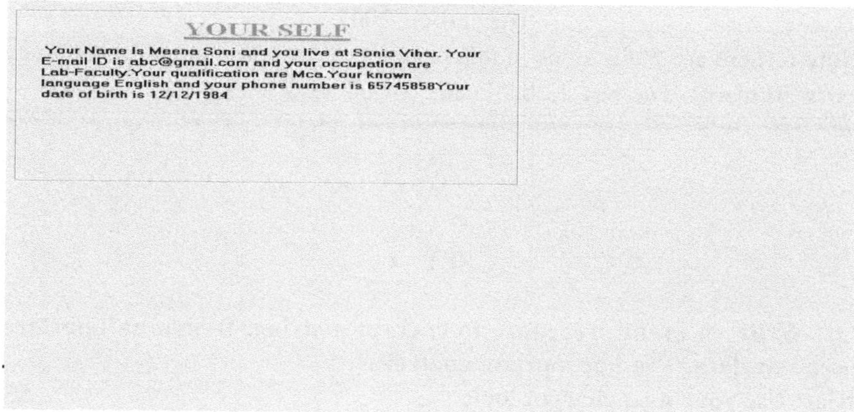

Code

```
Private Sub Command1_Click ()
frmSplash.Label2.Caption = “Your Name Is” & Text1.Text & “and you live at” & Text2.Text & “. Your E-mail ID is “ & Text3.Text & “and your occupation are” & Text4.Text & “.Your qualification are” & Text5.Text & “.Your known language” & Text6.Text & “and your phone number is “& Val (Text7.Text) & “Your date of birth is” & Text8.Text
frmSplash.Show
End sub
```

CS-65 : Windows Programming
December, 2007

Note : There are 2 questions in this paper. Answer both the questions. They carry 50 marks. The rest 25 marks are for the viva-voce.

SET - 1

Q1. Write an event procedure to encrypt a string. Design an interface user interface. Use appropriate controls.
Hint: Use your own encrypt logic **25**
Ans. Design Window

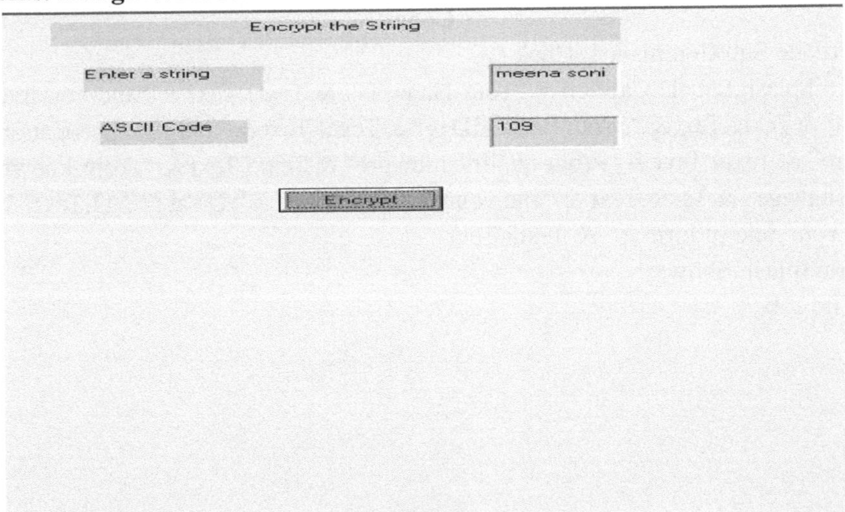

CODE

```
Private Sub Encrypt Click ()
Dim a As String
a = txt_str.Text
Txt_ecypt = Asc (a)
End Sub
```

Q2. Write an event procedure to generate a bill for a readymade garment store. Assumptions can be made wherever necessary. **25**
Ans. Design Window

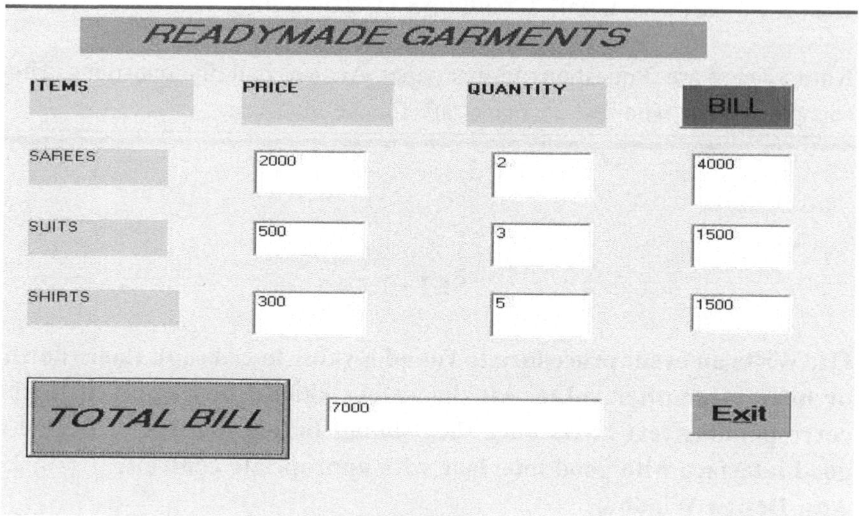

CODE

```
Private Sub Command1_Click ()
Text7.Text = Text1.Text * Text4.Text
Text8.Text = Text2.Text * Text5.Text
Text9.Text = Text3.Text * Text6.Text
End Sub

Private Sub Command2_Click ()
Text10.Text = Val (Text7.Text) + Val (Text8.Text) + Val (Text9.Text)
End Sub

Private Sub Command3_Click ()
End
End Sub
```

CS-65 : Windows Programming
December, 2007

Note : There are 2 questions in this paper. Answer both the questions. They carry 50 marks. The rest 25 marks are for the viva-voce.

SET - 2

Q1. Write an event procedure to round a value to ceil (up), floor (down) or near to another value. All the values should be displayed in the corresponding text boxes once the "submit button is pressed. Design a good interface with good interface with appropriate controls. 25

Ans. Design Window

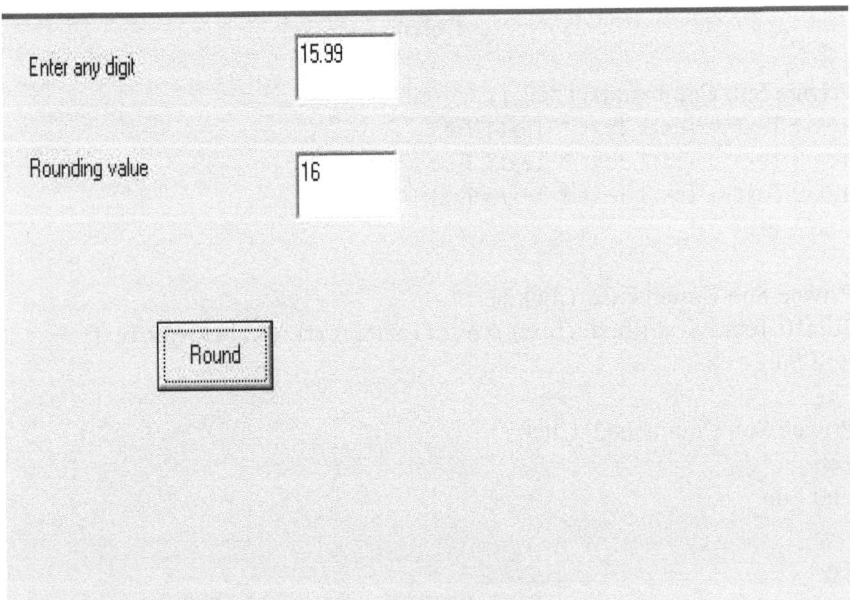

CODE

```
Private Sub Rnd_Click ()
Dim a As Integer
a = Txt_dig.Text
Round (a)
```

```
Txt_val.Text = a
End Sub
```

Q2. Write a vb application to add two matrices of size m*n and display the resultant matrix. Give you application a splash screen also. 25

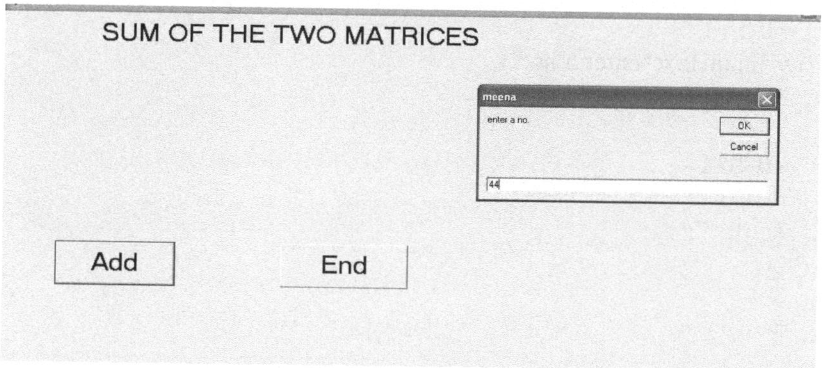

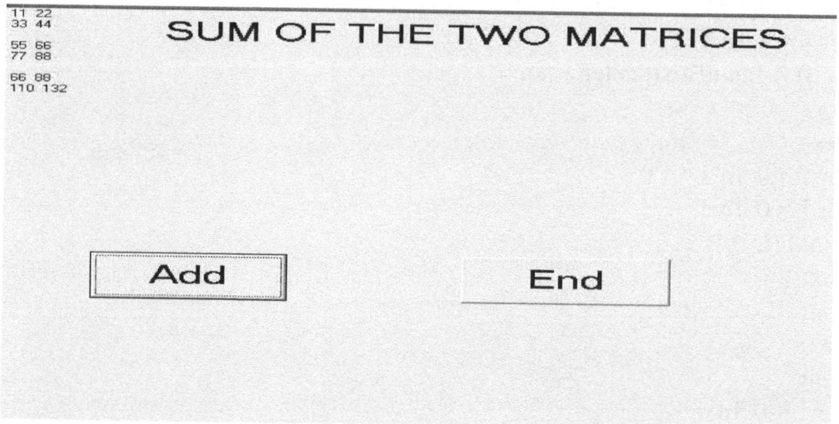

COMPONENT	COMPONENT NAME	COMPONENT USE
LABEL	LABEL1	SHOW THE RESULT
COMMAND	COMMAND1	SHOW THE OUTPUT
COMMAND	COMMAND2	FOR EXIT

PROPERTIES :

LABEL. CAPTION = "SUM OF TWO MATRICES
COMMAND1 CAPTION = " ADD"
COMMAND2 CAPTION = "END"

CODE SEGMENT:

```
Dim a(2, 2) As Integer
Dim b(2, 2) As Integer
Dim s(2, 2) As Integer
Private Sub Command1_Click()
For i = 0 To 1
For j = 0 To 1
a(i, j) = InputBox("enter a no.")
Next
Next
For i = 0 To 1
For j = 0 To 1
Print a(i, j); "";
Next
Print
Next
Print
For i = 0 To 1
For j = 0 To 1
b(i, j) = InputBox("enter a no.")
Next
Next
For i = 0 To 1
For j = 0 To 1
Print b(i, j); "";
Next
Print
Next
Print
For i = 0 To 1
For j = 0 To 1
s(i, j) = a(i, j) + b(i, j)
Print s(i, j); "";
Next
Print
Next
Print
End Sub
Private Sub Command2_Click()
End
End Sub
```

CS-65 : Windows Programming
December, 2007

Note : There are 2 questions in this paper. Answer both the questions. They carry 50 marks. The rest 25 marks are for the viva-voce.

SET - 3

Q1. Write an event procedure to count the number of blanks, tabs and new line character in a given string. Use appropriate controls and provide a user friendly interface.

Ans. Design Window

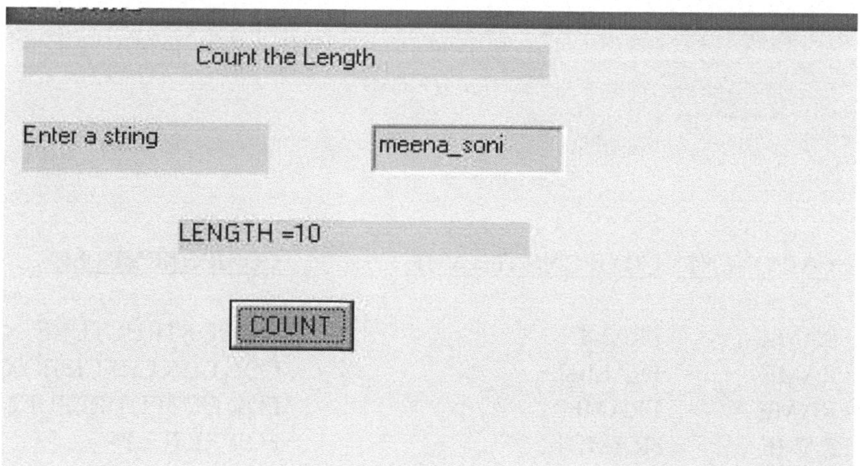

CODE

```
Private Sub Cmd_count_Click ()
Dim a As String
a = Txtlen.Text
Length. Caption = "LENGTH =" & Len (a)
End Sub
```

Q2. Create a VB application to generate a bill for a departmental store which sells electrical goods, electronics,garments,stationary,provisions etc. Give your application a splash screen also. Create a very good user GUI with appropriate controls. 25

Ans. Design Window

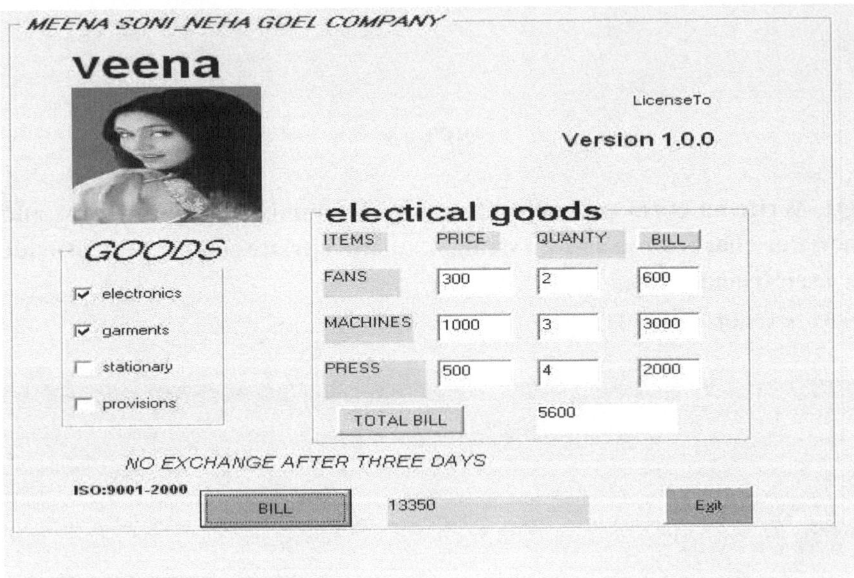

COMPONENT	COMPONENT NAME	COMPONENT USE
FRAME	FRAME1	STORE THE STRUCTURE
FRAME	FRAME2	CONTAIN CHECK BOX
FRAME	FRAME3	FOR OUTPUT RESULT
FRAME	FRAME4	FOR RESULT
PICTURE BOX	IMGLOGO	CONTAIN A PICTURE
LABEL	LABEL1	FOR COMMENT
LABEL	LABEL2	FOR COMMENT
LABEL	LABEL3	FOR COMMENT
LABEL	LABEL4	FOR COMMENT
LABEL	LABEL5	FOR COMMENT
TEXT	TEXT1	DISPLAY OUTPUT
TEXT	TEXT2	DISPLAY OUTPUT
TEXT	TEXT3	DISPLAY OUTPUT

TEXT	TEXT4	DISPLAY OUTPUT
TEXT	TEXT5	DISPLAY OUTPUT
TEXT	TEXT6	DISPLAY OUTPUT
TEXT	TEXT7	DISPLAY OUTPUT
TEXT	TEXT8	DISPLAY OUTPUT
TEXT	TEXT9	DISPLAY OUTPUT
TEXT	TEXT10	DISPLAY OUTPUT
TEXT	TEXT11	DISPLAY OUTPUT
TEXT	TEXT12	DISPLAY OUTPUT
TEXT	TEXT13	DISPLAY OUTPUT
TEXT	TEXT14	DISPLAY OUTPUT
TEXT	TEXT15	DISPLAY OUTPUT

PROPERTIES:

FRAME2	CAPTION = "ELECTRONIC GOODS"
FRAME2	CAPTION = "GARMENT STORE"
PICTURE BOX	PICTURE ="LOCATION OF PICTURE"
LABEL1	CAPTION = "LICENSE TO"
LABEL2	CAPTION = "VERSION-6.0"
LABEL3	CAPTION = "NO EXCHANGE AFTER 3 DAYS"
LABEL4	CAPTION = "ISO:9001-2000"
LABEL5	CAPTION = "VISUAL BASIC"
TEXT1	TEXT = " "
TEXT2	TEXT = " "
TEXT3	TEXT = " "
TEXT4	TEXT = " "
TEXT5	TEXT = " "
TEXT6	TEXT = " "
TEXT7	TEXT = " "
TEXT8	TEXT = " "
TEXT9	TEXT = " "
TEXT10	TEXT = " "
TEXT11	TEXT = " "
TEXT12	TEXT = " "
TEXT13	TEXT = " "
TEXT14	TEXT = " "

TEXT15 TEXT = " "

CODE

```
Private Sub Check1_Click ()
Frame3.Visible = True
Frame4.Visible = False
End Sub

Private Sub Check2_Click ()
Frame4.Visible = True
Frame3.Visible = False
End Sub

Private Sub Command2_Click ()
Text7.Text = Text1.Text * Text4.Text
Text8.Text = Text2.Text * Text5.Text
Text9.Text = Text3.Text * Text6.Text
End Sub
Private Sub Command3_Click ()
End
End Sub

Private Sub Command5_Click ()
Label14.Caption = Val (Text20.Text) + Val (Text21.Text) + Val (Text22.Text)
End Sub

Private Sub Command7_Click ()
End
End Sub
```

CS-65 : Windows Programming
December, 2007

Note : There are 2 questions in this paper. Answer both the questions. They carry 50 marks. The rest 25 marks are for the viva-voce.

SET - 4

Q1. Write an event procedure to find and display the rightmost occurrence of an input character of an n-length string. **25**

Ans. Design Window

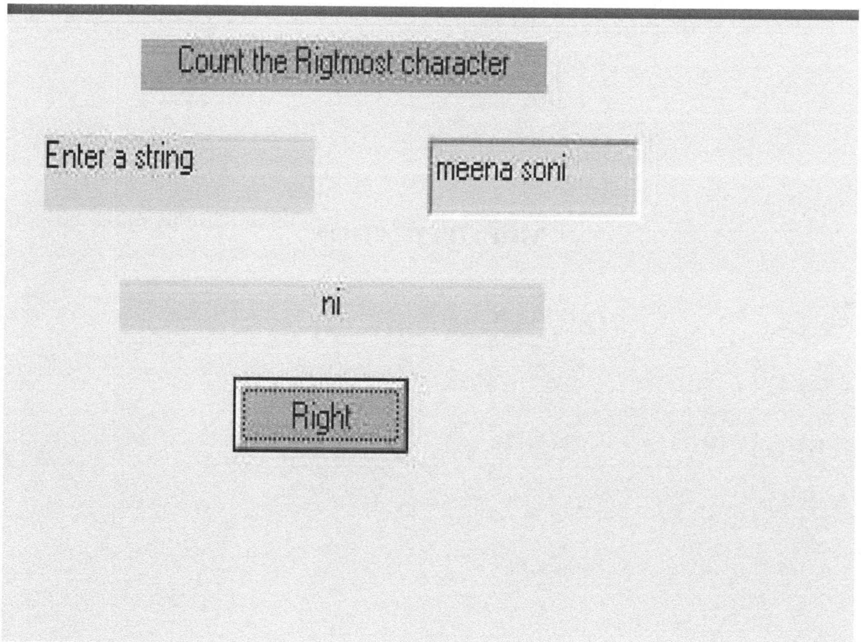

CODE

```
Private Sub Cmd_right_Click ()
Dim a As String
a = Txtrt.Text
Lblrt.Caption = Right (a, 2)
End Sub
```

Q2. Write a vb application to multiply two matrices of size m*n and n*m respectively. Create a good user interface for taking-in the elements of matrices and displaying them. 25

Ans. Design Window

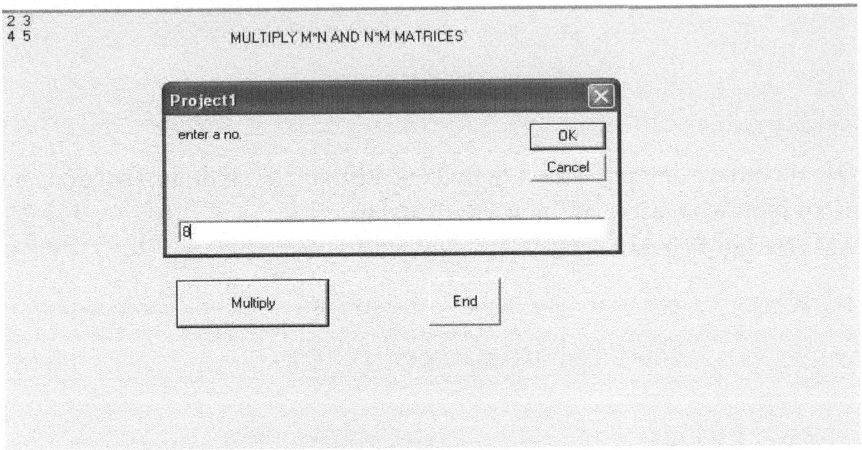

MULTIPLICATION

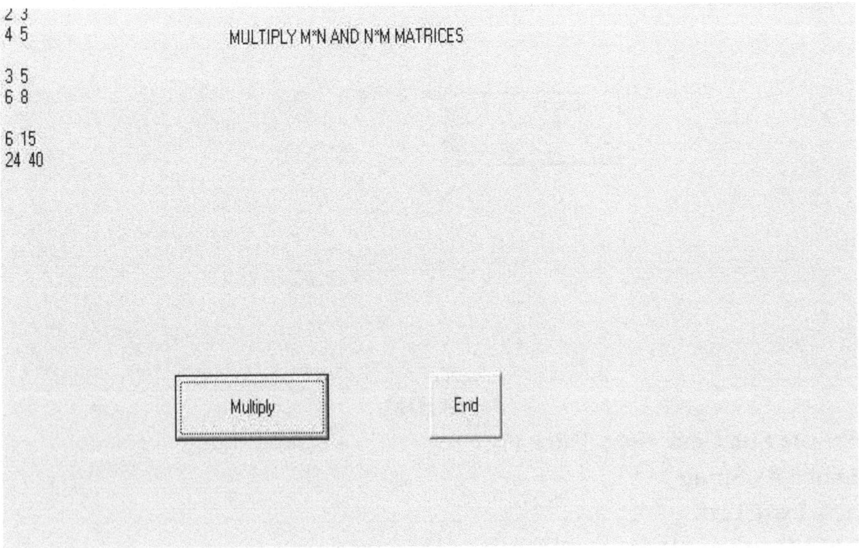

CS-65P : WINDOWS PROGRAMMING
June, 2008(Set-1)

Q1. Create a VB application to calculate the student's total marks In 5 courses. Each course consists of Assignment (Internal) and term-end examination components.
Assignment Is for 25 marks and term-end examination is for 75 marks. Pass in each component is compulsory and is 50% in order to declare the student successful in the course. Find the advantage and also percentage. Place the grade as per the following details.

Grade A :	**Percentage> 80%**
Grade A :	**Between 70% and 80%**
Grade B :	**Between 60% and 70%**
Grade C :	**Between 50% and 60%**
Fail :	**Percentage < 50 %**

Also design a splash screen. Select and place appropriate controls on the form to provide user friendly interface.

Q2. Create a VB application to count the number of occurrences of each vowel in the given string.
Sample output :
Input string : Technology
No. of occurrences of a = 0
e = 1
i = 0
o = 2
u = 0

CS-65P : WINDOWS PROGRAMMING
June, 2008 (Set -2)

Q1. Create a VB application to simulate a simple calculator to perform the arithmetic operations like addition, subtraction, multiplication, division and finding out percentage. Select and place appropriate control on the form to provide user-friendly interface.

Q2. Create a menu similar to that of a note-pad application using menu-editor.

Note : **No need to doing any programming.**

CS-65P : WINDOWS PROGRAMMING
June, 2008 (Set -3)

Q1. Create a VB application to calculate and display the Gross-pay, Deductions and the Net-pay for the employees of the company, given the Basic-pay, TA, DA, perks, HRA and deductions (GPF, medical contribution, pension scheme, loans). The pay-slip should consist of all the details of the employees along with the pay-details. Consider the following details for calculating the DA, HRA, perks, allowances.

TA = Rs/ 800/- for all the employees
DA = 40% Basic Pay
Perks = 9% Basic Pay
HRA = 30% of Basic Pay

Q2. Create a VB application to check whether the given string is a palindrome or not.

CS-65P : WINDOWS PROGRAMMING
June, 2008 (Set -4)

Q1. Create a simple application to simulate the billing system for an automobile spare parts shop. Also design the splash for this application. The UI Should be user-friendly with appropriate controls.

Q2. Create a VB application which will display the string-length for a given string.

CS-65P : WINDOWS PROGRAMMING
December, 2008 (Set-1)

Q1. Create simple VB application to simulate the billing system for a Grocery Shop. Also design the splash screen for this application. The user interface should be user-friendly with appropriate controls. The bill also should consist of the date and time.

Q2. Create a VB application to place three command buttons on the form, clicking upon which respective colour named on the command button should be displayed as the background colour of the form.

CS-65P : WINDOWS PROGRAMMING
December, 2008 (Set-2)

Q1. Create a simple VB application to count the number of occurrences of English articles (a, an, the) in a given statement.

Sample output:

Input String: A book is on the table.

No. of Occurrences of: "a"=1 time
"an"=0 times
"the"=1 time

Q2. Design a simple VB application to simulate a menu similar to that of MS-Paint application.

Note: No need of doing any programming.

CS-65P : WINDOWS PROGRAMMING
December, 2008 (Set-3)

Q1. Create a VB application to generate the bill for a post-paid mobile connection as per the details given below:

Rental charges	: Rs. 444/- (Monthly)
Free calls	: 100 calls (each call of 1 minute)
Local call	: Rs. 1/- per call (per minute)
STD	: Rs. 1.25/- per call (per minute)
ISD	: Rs. 8/- per call (per minute)
SMS	: Rs. 0.50 per (30 characters) SMS
Service Tax	: 2% of the amount

Also design a user friendly interface with appropriate controls.

Q2. Create a VB application to generate Fibonacci series of first 10 terms.

CS-65P : WINDOWS PROGRAMMING
December, 2008 (Set-4)

Q1. Create VB application to simulate a simple electronic voting machine to accept "n" no. of votes by the user and place the appropriate controls to declare the results after the voting time is over.

Note: Design an user friendly interface with appropriate controls...

Q2. Create VB application to generate random lines upon clicking the left mouse button of the mouse.

CS-65P : WINDOWS PROGRAMMING
June, 2009(Set-1)

Q1. Create a VB application to simulate the billing system for a sports stores. Also, design the splash screen for this application. Design the user interface with appropriate controls. The bill should consists of the date and time.

Q2. Create a VB application to generate random lines with different colours upon the mouse-over on the form. Place an "EXIT" button to close the application.

CS-65P : WINDOWS PROGRAMMING
June, 2009 (Set-2)

Q1. Create a VB application to simulate calculator. Place appropriate controls on the user interface.

Q2. Design a simple VB application to simulate a menu similar to that of "NOTE PAD" application.

Note: No need of doing any programming. Just design the menu/sub menu.

CS-65P : WINDOWS PROGRAMMING
June, 2009 (Set-3)

Q1. Create a VB application to count and print the no. of vowels in a given string.

Q2. Create a simple VB application to print the lucky number, if the birth_date is given as input. Design an attractive and user friendly interface with appropriate controls.

Simple Output :

Input : Birth date : 04-11-1982.
0+4+1+1+1+9+8+2
=26=2+6=8

Output : 8

CS-65P : WINDOWS PROGRAMMING
June, 2009 (Set-4)

Q1. Create a VB application to simulate the billing system for a "music stores" which sells Audio/Video CD's, DVD's, iPOD's and other accessories. Also, design the splash screen for this application. Design the interface with appropriate controls.

Q2. Write an event procedure to find the largest number among the three numbers given as input.